DUFFER'S BREAKTHROUGH: To Quit or to Quest

The plight of two duffers who, discouraged with their game, distill the galaxy of golf swing tips to a functional few with remarkable success.

By Rex Coryell

GOLF FOUNDATION OF WISCONSIN / FIRST TEE

For book ordering information

www.gfw.org

Phone: (414) 540-3830

FAX: 414.540.3831

Copyright 2000. The Golf Foundation of Wisconsin

All rights reserved. Except for quotes used in reviews, articles, or other media, no part of this book may be reproduced or transmitted by any form or by any means, electronic, or mechanical including photocopying, recording, or by information storage or retrieval system, without permission by The Golf Foundation of Wisconsin.

The Golf Foundation of Wisconsin
8989 N. Port Washington Rd.
Milwaukee, WI 53217
andrea.urban@gfw.org
(414) 540-3830
Fax 414.540.3831
Website: *www.gfw.org*

ISBN 0-9701183-0-9

Printed in the United States of America

Cover design by Bill Eisner

Dedication

To Harold Tritton, who is enjoying daily outings with his Creator and Mentor on a course free of hazards, bunkers, and undulated greens.

Clearly, Harold's reaction to any formal elegy would not be appreciated. He would say, "Scratch the epitaph to your old golfing partner! Just tell duffers everywhere to unlink their handicaps from their egos. Tell them to enjoy the game to the fullest, but be sure, when stepping off the 18th green, they resume life's more important games with an aggressive swing, sights on the right target, and focused execution."

Harold viewed the game of golf as a metaphor for the game of life, demanding of self-discipline, respect for others, patience, and setbacks balanced with successes. He would want – indeed insist – that any proceeds of this documentary be channeled to endeavors aimed at broadening the opportunities for this " game of life" to those otherwise out of reach. What more enduring endeavor than the Golf Foundation of Wisconsin/First Tee-Wisconsin?

*Founded in 1978, **GFW** (now partnered with First Tee) is dedicated to the expansion of the golfing experience through programs for minorities, physically challenged, learning-disabled, and those otherwise not able to afford or access the sport. Through instruction/mentoring programs, partnerships with school systems, and industry, there are opportunities for youth to learn essential life-long lessons and diverse skill-sets.*

The author and The Golf Foundation of Wisconsin/First Tee, the book's sponsor, wish to thank Associated Banc-Corp for underwriting the initial publishing costs, and for that corporation's commitment to the programs to which the book's proceeds are dedicated.

FOREWORD

Like many golfers who struggle with their games from time to time, I am always interested in the latest fads, theories, and observations about the golf swing. To that end, my personal collection of golf instructional books numbers in the hundreds. I must confess, many of these books are sent to me by publicists, who implore me to review them for readers of the *Milwaukee Journal Sentinel*. Truth is, I'd have purchased most of them anyway. It's a sickness.

The author list of these golf how-to books includes a litany of great players, such as Ben Hogan, Jack Nicklaus, Tom Watson, Seve Ballesteros, and Nick Faldo. And, of course, virtually every "name" teaching professional has used this venue to unlock the mysteries of the swing for us poor 5- and 25- handicappers.

From Hogan's immensely valuable *The Modern Fundamentals of Golf* to John Daly's *Grip It and Rip It*! virtually every facet of the swing has been explored, explained, analyzed and illustrated.

So when Steve Quale, executive director of the Golf Foundation of Wisconsin / First Tee, told me about someone hoping to add to this immense body of work, I was skeptical. I had never heard of Rex Coryell. He was neither a player of note nor a nationally known teacher of the golf swing. What could he possibly have to say that would be useful?

The answer, I found out, was "plenty."

As I read through a rough draft of *Duffer's Breakthrough*, I was struck by Coryell's common-sense approach. He tells the true story of two senior golfers, both high-handicappers, who seek to improve through a sort of collaborative mentoring.

Some might see this as a case of the "blind leading the blind." But, really, it makes perfect sense. After all, if everyone could "Golf My Way" (Nicklaus), the instructional golf book/video/ magazine market would dry up, because we'd all play to scratch.

The game's great players and teachers undoubtedly know what they're talking about. Unfortunately, few of us can get our bodies to do what theirs do. This is especially true of higher-handicappers, who may have physical limitations or cannot put in hours of practice...or who may be just plain confused. But "Duffer's Breakthrough" offers proof that they can help one another.

The protagonists apply the "Pareto Principle" to golf learning, using trial and error to identify a handful of imageries that work for them. They dismiss the techniques and tips that do not help, thus avoiding the bane of all hackers: Paralysis by analysis. The beauty of this methodology is that, although readers may want to apply the final "picks" to their games, they should feel encouraged to come up with their own.

It's the process that counts.

The information in this book does indeed have value. More than that, however, I have found Rex Coryell to be a warm and engaging human being whose generosity must not go unmentioned. He has insisted on donating all proceeds from the sale of *Duffer's Breakthrough* to the Golf Foundation of Wisconsin / First Tee.

Here's hoping you experience a "breakthrough" in your own games.

                                        Gary D'Amato

CONTENTS

Dedication		*i*
Foreword		*iii*
Introduction		5
Chapter 1	Whether to Quit or to Quest	7
Chapter 2	Advice from the Doctor	21
Chapter 3	Skateboarding with a Reverse K	28
Chapter 4	Disciplining the Elbows	32
Chapter 5	The Perception-Reality Gap	43
Chapter 6	The Electrified, Petrified Left Wrist	49
Chapter 7	Advancement to C Division	58
Chapter 8	The Short Game	60
Chapter 9	Pareto's Final Picks	64
Chapter 10	Golf and the Out-of-Body Experience	80
Chapter 11	Nirvana and Goals Reviewed	85
Epilogue		90
Acknowledgment		*93*
About the Author		*95*

INTRODUCTION

No doubt there are tens of thousands of weekend golfers who experience only the joy of the game, oblivious to any agitation over the botched shot, the lost ball, and the astronomical score. These carefree and blithe spirits are to be admired, indeed envied. Yet, there are equally as many of us duffers who allow the hates in our *love-hate* relationship with the game to outweigh the joys. The frequent disconnect between clubhead and ball is the source of deep-seated frustration, embarrassment, angst, and, yes, depreciated self-image.

It is this latter community of golfers who will identify with this true account of two duffers, who, after a season of outings in a senior men's golf league, become hopelessly discouraged. Attempts at improvement through instruction had led to a plethora of *dos* and *don'ts* that proved more confusing than constructive. After confessing harbored feelings of humiliation, they embark upon a plan of "bootstrap improvement," with the pledge that unless certain specified results are achieved in three months, all golf equipment will be turned over to the church rummage sale, and any further thoughts of the sport abandoned.

Their strategy for improving the golf swing employs Pareto's "80-20" principle of identifying and intensifying the handful of swing techniques having the greatest impact on results. The two commit to researching instructional materials and to the trial-and-error testing of discoveries at their bi-weekly "bootstrap clinics." The idea that students can learn from each other proves out. But equally important as the dramatically improved handicaps are the feelings of fulfillment and enjoyment in a game previously fraught with frustration.

***Duffers Breakthrough*, therefore, is right at the intersection of two landmark observations about the game of golf:** First, "The average golfer is capable of building a repeating swing and breaking 80 if he learns a *small number* of correct movements." (Ben Hogan). And second, "Golf is a game that tests you as a person far more than it tests you as an athlete." (Tommy Bolt).

The hurried reader primarily interested in swing mechanics may wish to zoom in on those pages containing illustrations, where the discovery of each clinic is highlighted. Then in Chapter 9 (*Pareto's Final Picks*) he/she can find a handy reference which recaps those swing techniques making up the "final selection."

Other readers, however, will choose to relive the process employed by Harold and myself as we derived the *breakthrough* golf swing. They will experience the poignantly human story of two acquaintances who become the closest of friends through the shared emotional and experiential continuum of despair and exasperation, exploration and goals-setting, resolve and collaborative mentoring, and finally, confidence restored and celebration.

The book holds a special appeal for high-and mid-handicappers who are frustrated with their level of play, persons with the desire to take up golf who perceive themselves too busy for the traditional start-up methodology, and those golfers who are victims of the (widespread) "crush- the-ball syndrome."

"A bad attitude is worse than a bad swing."
—Payne Stewart

CHAPTER 1

Whether to Quit or to Quest

Harold Trittin and I were not exempt from the universality of Raymond Floyd's insightful lament, *"The game of golf was easy for me as a kid, but I had to play a while to find out how hard it is."*

Indeed, the game of golf *did* seem easy to Hal and I at an early age as we experimented in the backyards of our homes with dust-covered, wood-shafted clubs that had been sleeping in the furthest reaches of the basement. Both of us were sufficiently beguiled by the euphoria of the occasional sweet shot to venture forth to the nearest public course with neighborhood friends. Unencumbered with the self-consciousness and embarrassment that would plague us in later years, we routinely pierced the "one hundred" scoring barrier with minimal thought to its significance.

For Harold, these childhood golfing encounters took place in the community of Wausau, Wisconsin. About the same time, I was sporting my father's wood shafts the length of Indian Hills Golf Course in Grand Rapids, Michigan.

Perhaps Harold would have devoted more of his spare time to golf were it not for the advice of Ms. Easterday, a ninth grade teacher and self-appointed mentor, who urged him to dedicate more time to violin lessons, poetry, and art. She insisted it was important to develop his "right brain" potential. (The violin caught on, but the art and poetry were later dropped.)

And in my case, it was cornet lessons and academics that kept me from honing my golfing skills in adolescent years. My high school counselor convinced me that to achieve a boyhood dream of a Congressional appointment to the United States Naval Academy, it was imperative to sustain a straight A record. (Actually, the appointment was earned with only a B+ record).

Five decades later, the two of us became acquainted at a couples' discussion group in a church in Fox Point, Wisconsin. At the time, Harold was a bank executive and I was a senior associate for a firm that facilitated executive education and personal counseling for CEOs. We both were contemplating retirement, and though golf had been only an occasional— sometimes obligatory— activity in our adult lives, the idea of golfing regularly was now doable, and perhaps desirable. Together with wives, Ethel and Patti, we spent an occasional evening together which afforded the opportunity to discuss the next chapter in our lives. Anxious to avoid the mental and physical meltdown often associated with male retirement, we committed to a specific plan of volunteer pursuits and to regular golf outings. The dual objective was societal "give-back" and outdoor recreation.

It was a year later that Harold learned about the Brown Deer Park Men's Golf League, which appeared to provide a low-budget opportunity to participate in a form of no-stress competition in the context of active fellowship. We were attracted to the idea of playing Brown Deer. Nature had endowed this beautiful park with the area's finest hardwood trees, challenging hills, and a winding stream that both danced and laughed — especially, when tickled by errant golf balls. Having recently been designated the venue for the Greater Milwaukee Open, the floral treatments, fairways, bunkers, and greens were the beneficiary of Milwaukee County's intensive efforts to elevate this facility to world-class status, an effort soon to be rewarded by national ranking.

Now, into the second year of this competitive involvement, we found the objective of fellowship was being met, but other objectives, such as sharing in the prize money, (which titillated twenty percent of the participants), and improving upon our embarrassingly high handicaps (mid-forties), continued to allude us.

****

I stared down the fairway of the par-5 fourth hole as I was addressing my Top-Flite, and swung for all I was worth.

For two precious seconds, everything was fine. The ball shot from the clubface and seemed intent on finding the middle of the fairway. Then, in mid-flight, it apparently changed its mind, as golf balls sometimes do. Some 50 yards past the forward tees, the ball took a right turn and headed for cover in the woods.

"Can you believe it?" I said in exasperation. "The widest fairway on the course, and I manage to slice it into the shrubs way over to the right!"

Harold Trittin, my playing partner for the league's 16-week competition, squinted as the ball disappeared into the foliage. A couple of falling leaves marked its entrance into the woods; the sharp crack of Top-Flite off wood told both of us that it might be difficult to locate.

"Didn't see where it landed, Rex," Harold said hopefully, "but I'm sure we'll find it."

Shaking my head I slammed the driver back into the bag.

"I don't understand it, Hal. Last night I was seven for ten in decent drives at the driving range and now, in the real world, I'm more like one in ten! Must be something to do with the whole world gazing at the posted scores. Why should that bug me so much? Why should that distract my concentration and decimate my game? Here's the painful reality: I'm into three-digit scores *whether or not* it's competition golf. Disgusting!"

"You're too hard on yourself, Rex. You have natural athletic ability. Others we've been paired with comment on that. Besides, you're fun to play with at these forays. I personally enjoy your company, and I enjoy the beauty of this place. Hate to see you get so down on yourself."

"I appreciate that, Hal, I really do. But I wonder sometimes if the fellowship and the scenic stroll is worth the humiliation of making an ass of one's self— to say nothing of the permanent damage to the self-esteem. As to the natural athletic ability, that's strictly external. What others don't see is the confusion inside my head. In the interlude of a two-second swing my computer's feverishly scanning every *should* and *shouldn't* I've ever been taught. The result is usually a death-grip twisting of the hands which throws the clubhead out of alignment...big time!"

"All the time we've been playing together I had no idea you harbored that level of frustration with your game. How long has this been going on?"

"Sorry to burden you with my golfing woes, Hal. The others are waiting for me to *punch* this ball out of these bushes. For now, let's both focus on taking 'dead aim,' as Harvey Penick would say, and then, in the clubhouse, we'll do a pathology on my late-life golfing crisis....over an extra donut."

We played the rest of the course with less than the usual banter and kibitzing. I was unable to shake the blues I was feeling over my inability to perform to what I knew to be a higher potential. Part of me was hoping Hal would not bring up the subject of this deep and personal disappointment during our habitual post-game, post-mortems in the clubhouse lounge.

"So, let's ask the question again," Harold queried, as he quickly snatched the tab from the waiter. "How long have you been on the edge of jettisoning this crazy game? And let me add upfront that I've been struggling with a similar kind of question, so I'm genuinely interested in knowing where your head, heart, and spleen are at on this issue."

"This kind of self-disclosure doesn't come easy, Hal, but here goes. At the risk of sounding arrogant let me lay out what I've always thought to be a pretty decent track record of eye-hand coordination. As an Eagle Scout — surely you're excited to hear this slice of ancient history — I was the first in my troop to earn the hat trick of physical fitness, athletics, and life saving merit badges. Later at Annapolis, I enjoyed sports and was considered to be very competitive in intramural tennis, gymnastics, and squash. Would you believe I was captain of a make-up team which held the 'mids' of the Royal Naval College to a draw at their own sport of cricket?"

"I'm impressed," Hal marveled, tongue in cheek. "Keep going."

"It gets better. I can back a boat trailer the length of a driveway without stopping. And at our island cottage, I regularly land a twenty-foot day sailer at a precise point on the dock in adverse wind conditions and among boat-eating boulders. Furthermore, if you can stand any more of this neuro-muscular trivia, just fifty feet from that dock I regularly enhance my ego by swinging an axe with near perfect precision. Even the split logs snap to attention out of respect for my proficiency with an industrial size axe.

"Now," I continued, "does any of this carry over into a coordinated swing with a number 3-wood? No way!"

"I'm beginning to understand," Hal said. "But allow me an observation about your ability with the axe. I'm going to guess the action is mostly hands and arms, and the object is to acquire a near vertical drop without veering left or right."

"Essentially you're right," I said.

"Contrast that level of eye-hand coordination to what you already know about the textbook golf swing," reasoned Hal. "The power generator is the legs and hips with the arms and clubshaft merely dragging along for the ride. Not that I'll ever master this athletic anomaly, but I've been told this is the only hope for a sweet connection between clubface and ball — the perfect swing you and I keep searching for. Think about the countless opportunities for the clubface to stray one millimeter from perfect square with the ball.

That's lot different from the swing of an axe handle, or for all I know, the manipulation of the cricket paddle."

"If I read you, Hal, anyone attempting to master the golf swing is facing a foe so complex, so daunting...."

"More than daunting," interrupted Harold, "downright terrorizing! Let me ask if you've thought through any objectives for your golf improvement?"

"Interesting you should ask. Just last night I was reviewing some goals with Patti, who was wondering how long I intend to endure this punishment. I shared with her my immediate goal of breaking out of the D Division of this senior's golf league. After all, the average player is ten years my senior — as in the Golden Pond genre. There's two chaps at the table behind you that are definitely *beyond* geriatric. Certainly I should be in the C or B Division by this time.

"Another goal...and this goes back a couple of years to a retirement ceremony: I was deeply touched when a group of clients, all CEOs, presented me with an embarrassingly generous gift certificate for what they labeled 'no-excuse golf clubs.' In the banter that followed I promised to lower my handicap by ten strokes! That seemed like a reasonable goal, and I took that commitment very seriously. So now, two years and one set of Wilson graphites later, my handicap is down a full stroke. Oh yes, factor eight golf lessons into that equation! You can imagine how the conversation goes every time I run into one of those benefactors. My handicap gets discussed as if it were a mutual friend with a terminal illness."

Whether to Quit or to Quest

"Yeah, you do have goals, Rex. Unrealized, maybe, but very clear goals."

I continued. "Now here's one I didn't share with Patti, and it seems to be the most unattainable goal of them all. It relates to the swing of the axe handle. You've heard me talk about son Eric, the scratch golfer?"

"Yes," said Harold. "I just assumed that any family with five sons must have a resident scratch golfer."

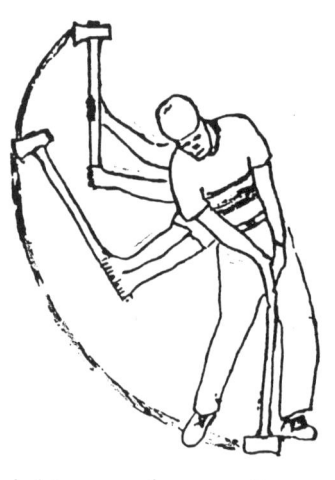

"Well," I said, "not long ago, he and I were reviewing a video of my golf swing, and his comment was, 'You're doing fine, Dad, but doesn't it seem to you that you're all arms?' He's dead right, you know. I *am* all arms. There's this demonic inner voice that tells me this is a sledgehammer and that I must launch that ball at Warp 7 speed. Believe me when I tell you I have no other addictions. But there is this one uncontrollable habit — perhaps it's an adrenaline rush — which overrides every discipline and impels me to blister that ball! The result, of course, is the botched shot. The paradox here is that I'm not the kind of person who has to prove anything — especially something as macho as belting a little white ball into the next zip code. That's not the way I'm wired. So, it's clear to me my most immediate goal is to get rid of this addiction...this killer instinct. Unless I can accomplish this, there's no hope for the other goals. But enough of that! You alluded to something earlier about your own misgivings over this frustrating sport."

"Oh yeah." Hal paused to gather his thoughts. "Well, my grandson Jason, age 16, loves to take me golfing. And I mean it's *humbling*! Jason is not yet a scratch golfer but surely tracking to become one. It's not just Jason, it's my son-in-law, Paul. It's some neighbors I play with regularly. It's...you name it. Like you were saying, if there's no measurable improvement, one looks in the mirror and asks if this is a worthwhile expenditure of energy — unrewarded energy. But I can't isolate my problem to just the 'sledgehammer' syndrome. My golfswing problems vary all over the place. And the more instructions I get, the more the problems multiply.

"Another thing. You may have noticed the gimp in my right leg every time we descend a slope or set of stairs."

"Yes, I guess I have," I said.

"Well it's a degenerative knee. And though I try not to complain about it, there's a ton of pain with each descending step. So, at the beginning of each golfing season I have to ask myself if the satisfaction of the game is going to offset the pain in the knee."

"That's a rough one, Hal. What was the genesis of your knee problem?"

"An accident in flight training school, Randolph Field, just eight months after entering the Army Air Corps."

"C'mon. You're not that old!" I chided. "You're talking W.W.II?" `

"You've got it." Hal sighed. "You pointed out the two geriatrics a few minutes ago? Include *me* in that club."

"Let me quote my stepmother," I said. "At age 99 she's driving her car all over the city of Grand Rapids to play...correction...to *win* bridge competitions. She and John Glenn share the same mantra: 'Age is only an attitude.' "

Hal and I stared at each other for several moments. We shared a look that reflected a measure of despair, and also a measure of sympathy. It was as if a new level of understanding and compassion was emerging between us which would bond our friendship to a deeper and more devoted level.

"I would like to pose a proposition," said Hal, interrupting the long silence. "We're both motivated to improve our game. And short of improvement, we're both prepared to drop it forever."

"You've got that right!" I said.

"My take is we've both given up on whatever additional improvement may come from lessons."

"Yeah," I said. "Why is it that every pro I've been to promises in advance to build on the strengths I already have, then proceeds to re-engineer my stance and swing from toenail to fingernail? And why is it that no two of them agree on the same techniques for swing improvement?"

"Okay," Hal continued, "let's make a commitment to do research — instructional literature, books, videos, and so forth, and isolate the handful of techniques that we both agree are truly helpful. Then commit to working real hard on those essentials. Then, if there's no improvement by, let's say, mid-September, we donate our clubs to the church rummage sale and never pick up another golf club!"

I grimaced during an uncomfortably long silence. Finally I mumbled, "That scraping noise you hear is my Scottish spleen. Besides, these clubs were gifted to me; they represent icons in my life." Another pause.

"Okay, partner, it's Nike time. Let's 'just do it'!"

"I have to believe this thing's going to work," Hal asserted, "we're smart enough to zero in on those things which will really make a difference in our individual golf strokes. If not, we're at least smart enough to know when to call it quits when something ain't fixable. As Patti said to you, 'How long can we endure the pain?' "

"Suddenly I'm reminded of something that has relevance here," I interjected. "You've heard of the Pareto Principle?"

"The 80 - 20 thing?"

"That's it," I said, "I was at a seminar where the instructor asked some seasoned executives the same question. They were so insulted by the implication of their ignorance they didn't give him the courtesy of a reply. So, thinking none had ever heard of Pareto, he proceeded to give this lengthy explanation. And then, as if his audience were a group of high school freshmen, he asked: 'Now, can any of you think of a practical application of the Pareto Principle?' Immediately the class quipster raised his hand: 'Yes!!...I floss 20 percent of the time, and expect to save 80 percent of my teeth!' The place broke up!"

"That's hilarious! Was the seminar leader embarrassed?" Hal asked.

"Nah. He never got it. So, in his stuffy manner he went on to offer some of the more fundamental business examples, such as 20 percent of the customer base accounting for 80 percent of sales, and so forth. Anyway, would you agree that if Pareto were into golf he would argue that only 20 percent of all the *how to's* has any real significance and..."

"..the other 80 percent is garbage," finished Harold.

"Exactly! So, I'm suggesting that as you and I go about the task of locating those techniques of the swing that are really going to make a difference, we keep Velfrido Pareto in mind."

"Makes sense," agreed Hal. "Think about it! Ben Hogan must have had Velfrido Pareto in mind when he said, *'The average golfer is capable of building a repeating swing and breaking 80 if he learns a small number of correct movements.'* Now does that validate the 80-20 principle or what! As you say, our goal is to isolate those "few correct movements." Very heady stuff!!

"So Rex, what's your guess as to the number of high impact techniques we're likely to come up with?"

"How many H.I.T.s?" I queried.

"What?" Hal asked quizzically.

"You know, H.I.T.s – <u>H</u>igh <u>I</u>mpact <u>T</u>echniques!"

"Nice ring to it," Hal observed, "but let's not pollute our research with too many T.L.A.s"

"T.L.A.s?" I asked.

"Yeah, you know," Hal said. "<u>T</u>hree <u>L</u>etter <u>A</u>cronyms."

"I deserved that," I said. "To answer your question, it's my belief that exceeding seven is more than the average human can focus on."

"That's fine." Hal said. "I'm reminded of my last lesson when the pro said that with enough practice I should get the swing down to such an unconscious routine the mind thinks of *nothing...* none of the mechanics"

"Yeah, right!" I said frowning. "Let me tell you how easy it is for me to go through the entire backswing and downswing without once thinking about mechanics. It would be easier for me to listen to the entire refrain of the 'William Tell Overture' without *once* thinking about the Lone Ranger."

We both had a good laugh. Then we agreed that the number of 'Pareto picks' should not exceed eight. We committed to reviewing old issues of *Golf Digest,* which I had been squirreling for more than five years, and two-plus years accumulation of *Golf Magazine* and *Senior Golfer* in Hal's den. Our review would also include the scanning of golf how-to videos and books from a selection of more than 200 located in the network of Greater Milwaukee libraries. We also agreed to inquire of other golfers — both low- and high-handicappers — what essentials helped them the most in the development of the swing. Finally, we would select those tips that had the most meaning — particularly those that could be burned into memory-core with a sharp and lasting visual image.

"The swing is a sequence of awkward contortions designed to produce a graceful result." —Tommy Armour

CHAPTER 2

Advice from the Doctor

June 10th marked the next senior men's competition. One hour prior to our assigned tee time, Harold and I met at the older of two practice areas. Here we knew we would have a semblance of privacy to exchange information garnered during the previous two weeks.

"Hope you're armed with a winner," said Harold, as he greeted me, his newly appointed "research partner."

"Why me? I was counting on you to launch this new chapter in our lives. You know, some breakthrough insight that will guarantee a five-point handicap reduction!"

"C'mon, let's have it!" Harold insisted.

"Did a ton of reading and made lots of notes for future reference," I said. "Clearly, this is not a five-pointer, but the pay-off of the week for me was a productive conversation with Jeff Owens, my next-door neighbor."

"I recall your talking about him," said Hal. "The orthodontist who recently won the North Shore Club championship?"

"That's him. And a heck of a nice guy, by the way."

"Maybe so," Hal cautioned, "but if the meter was running during that consultation the per-minute rate of an orthodontist would have to get into big money!"

Advice from the Doctor

"Not to worry! The advice was in exchange for the loan of a fertilizer spreader. So...where to begin? Jeff is very much the gentleman. Anyone else would have scoffed at the notion of two duffers like us thinking we can help each other improve our handicaps. He avoided any reference to the 'blind leading the blind.' It was also comforting to hear him admit to an earlier period in his life when he suffered the same 'murder-the-ball' syndrome.

"Jeff convinced me that before there's any hope for change in muscle behavior, there has to be a fundamental 'paradigm shift.' With apologies for the big words. Eventually, some kind of repeated mantra penetrates deep enough to alter the mindset and drive a very different neuro-muscular behavior. In his opinion, the idea that the golf swing's a very natural thing is baloney.

"He says there are 64 seldom-used muscles that need to be synchronized into a sequence of unnatural movements, all in less then two seconds. Then, with countless rehearsals, this menagerie of movements finally meshes into an unconscious and fluid flow."

Harold mused, "I have a golf calendar that quotes Tommy Armour: *'The swing is an awkward sequence of bodily contortions designed to produce a graceful result.'* "

"Another thing," I continued, "Jeff says we need to decide first whether we are going to be 'swingers' or 'hitters.' "

"Swing whaaa?" Harold grunted.

"Yeh. Those golfers whose right side is dominant, i.e., right arm, right shoulder, upper torso, regard themselves as 'hitting' the ball. Clearly, I'm one of those. Anyway, those whose driving force is the lower torso — hips and legs — are the 'swingers.' After their rotating hips clear the way, the arms along with the clubshaft drag along for the ride — kind of what you were saying earlier. The consciousness of the swinger is not that of *hitting* the ball. Rather he is sweeping, or swinging *through*, the ball. He urges that we opt for 'swinger' even though this is probably the least natural of the two. It's the door to the more predictable and grooved swing."

Harold murmured, "I have to take a few seconds to visualize that one."

"As a matter of fact, you and I talked about the need to have a sharp visual that can be associated with each high-impact technique, or mantra, or whatever we're going to call it. We may have our first visceral visual from brother Owens!"

"Where do you find those big words?" Hal asked. "What's a visceral? Something to do with the gut?"

"Dunno for sure, but my gut says it is."

"Ye of big word and bad pun," said Hal

"So are you ready for this?" I asked.

Advice from the Doctor

"Swing!...er H.I.T.... er whatever!"

"Imagine you are at water's edge throwing a flat stone *underarm* with intent to generate as many skips as possible along the surface of the water. Go ahead and try it." I waited for Harold's execution. "Now, notice how your pelvis thrusts toward the intended line of flight long before your hands and arms come through for the final flick of the stone."

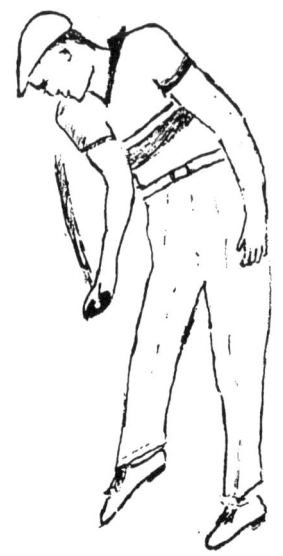

"Yup!" Hal exclaimed. "Very different from the proverbial swing of the axe. Here, the legs and hips are the engine. Even my feet feel like part of the engine. It's a new sensation. I like it!"

"Here's a reinforcer to that one," I continued. "Visualize your lower torso to be a heavy-duty, vertical crankshaft, or axle, rotating in a fixed barrel. It jump-starts from zero to 1,000 rpm in less than a second. The upper body, arms, hands, clubshaft are merely a limp and lifeless strip of leather with one end attached to the crankshaft and the other to the clubhead. They're like a tether whipping the clubhead along an orbital path...like the string that pulls the three-ounce weight of the yo-yo. And like the yo-yo, you're conscious of the weight of the clubhead in orbit, but not the 'lifeless tether' that's pulling it. I have to tell you, Hal, when I go through this drill at the range the result in control and distance is phenomenal!"

"Okay, what's your read on all this?" Harold asked.
"Do we have a winner? Is this our first mantra?"

"Why do I have a problem with the label 'mantra?' Anyway, I'm not quite ready to say this one qualifies, but clearly, there's something here! Maybe it's a case of determining which visualization *feels* better. And *your* reaction, sir?"

"I think it's got large potential. I'll check it out. Might even gin up the courage to try these visuals in today's game. If you hear me cursing, you know they're no help."

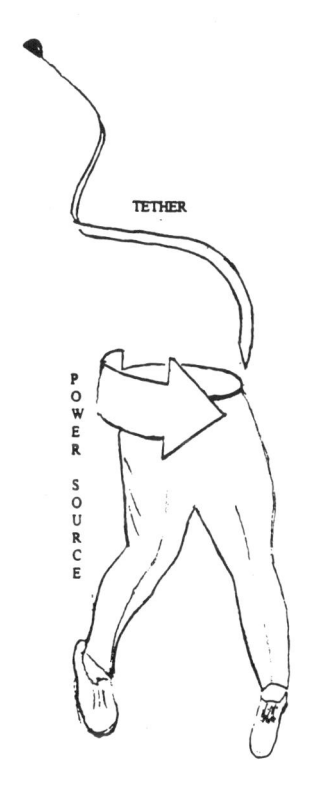

"Then you better not try today," I said. "I'd have to tell my neighbor I lost a good friend and golfing partner over his crummy advice."

"No way. Tell me, is this helping your crush-the-ball instinct?" Harold asked.

"Curiously, I feel myself undergoing a gradual adrenaline transfusion. There's less of a rush of energy to my arms and hands and more to the lower 'engine.' Of course that's where the source of power ought to be!" Then I paused before continuing.

"This gives me a flashback to the elder hostel experience of a year ago."

"The one in Carmel Valley with the former golf pro?"

"Right. Actually, as of last year, that pro...name's Ben Doyle...still held national ranking in *Golf Magazine*. So he made this big point about 'squeezing the buns' as you're about to strike the ball."

"You're joking." Hal exclaimed. "I'll bet that went over with the elder set."

"You're very perceptive," I said. "On day two the attendance plummeted...almost as much as the plunge in dignity of the little old ladies in high heels."

"Anyway," I continued, "because he never explained the *purpose* for 'squeezing the buns,' I never really got with the program. Now I'm beginning to realize that muscular maneuver adds a lot of power to the lower torso when most needed. With more practice I think I can transfer all my urge to power the swing from the arms to the squeezing the b....I prefer to call it, 'tucking the tush.' "

"How about 'gunning the gluterals'?" Hal joshed. "I find this *very* fascinating! Whether or not this one becomes a finalist, I have to believe we're going to find some good stuff in the reading materials which strongly reinforce the 'Owens Techniques.' "

"Yes, and we'll also find some stuff that contradicts them," I said. "It gets to me how much the pros that do books and videos have conflicting views on fundamental elements of the golf swing. Each sets himself up as the final word. The gospel according to — fill-in-the-blank."

I continued. "Think about it, good friend, now that we are 'writing the book,' it's *our* gospel, and we don't have to sweat the contradictions of the pros."

"Sounds sweet to me!" Hal said. "How do you like this book title?: *'Two Duffers' Perspectives on the Perfect Golf swing: Forget Everything You Ever Learned From the Pros.'*"

We laughed. Then Hal added, "How about, *'Golf for Dummies, by Two Dummies.'*" Our laughter grew to an hilarious outburst.

After a few moments of fantasizing about authoring a book, Harold put his arm around my shoulder to gesture the way to the first tee. After the round, we turned in the scores for posting and reviewed the highlights of our game – both the sweet and the sour. We agreed it had been another roller coaster of emotions, but confessed to a renewed sense of hope and promise — probably the result of our determination to "pursue a plan of positive improvements," as Hal termed it.

> *"Weekend golfers find it difficult to turn at the waist, particularly if there's a lot of waist to turn."*
> —Harry Vardon

CHAPTER 3

Skateboarding with a Reverse K

On June 24th both Hal and I appeared earlier than agreed, partly in our eagerness to share discoveries, and partly to seize the chance to brush-up ahead of the other's arrival. It was show 'n tell time, and, at the unconscious level, each of us wanted the other's approval over demonstrable progress.

"What a gorgeous morning!" I shouted while observing Harold limping down the hill toward the practice pitching area.

"No time for small talk!" retorted Harold. "Gotta tell you about the next Pareto Pick!"

"Tell me, tell me!"

"Skateboard!" Harold blurted out, hardly able to control his enthusiasm.

"That's it?" I asked in astonishment.

"Don't laugh. You won't believe how neatly this one piggybacks to the toss of the skipping stone!"

"Try me, I'll believe anything."

"This is authentic stuff," Harold said. "Right out of *Golf Digest*. Picture yourself balanced on a skateboard in your normal golf stance."

"Let me push the rewind button to my days with a skateboard," I chuckled.

"Now," Harold continued, "you start your backswing so smoothly the skateboard doesn't even move. Your hands are so quiet you don't dare twist the clubhead for the first 90 degrees of the backswing. But it's okay to gradually shift *all* your weight to your right leg. Then, as soon as your hands reach ear level, or whatever height suits you, *power-launch* the skateboard in the direction of the target! This means you've got to slam the weight of your entire body over to your *left* leg. In the process your hips and knees shift laterally — in the direction of the target."

"Hurry up! I'm about to fall off my skateboard!" I said.

Ignoring the interruption, Hal said, "Just because your lower torso has shifted laterally to the left doesn't mean you're allowed to sway your shoulders and head along with it. And by the way, your concentration is so focused on the kick-start of your feet, legs and hips, you haven't even *thought* about hands and arms. You know, they're the 'tether' that drags along behind the heavy-duty 'crankshaft,' the power source.

At the very last moment the wrists unhinge, but not before the hands reach level of right thigh. The tendency is to uncock the wrists too soon, which defeats everything else you're trying to do."

"Time out!" I exclaimed. "Let me try it a couple of times."

"Uh uh!" warned Harold. "Your head is lunging to the left too early. Your head can catch up to the rest of you *after* striking the ball! *Not before.*"

"Obviously, you think I'm some sort of contortionist!" I complained. "In the movie, "Star Wars" Obi-wan Kanobi tries to teach this movement to his protégé, Luke Skywalker. This is right after Luke learns to levitate and to activate objects from a distance. Turns out that levitating is *much* easier than the maneuver you're showing me!"

"I read you." Hal acknowledged. "But the good Doctor said it would feel unnatural at first. Consider this. The momentum of your hips and legs — 70 percent of your total mass — is so powerful you can physically have all your weight on your *left* leg while your head is still cocked back six inches to the *right* of the ball. It's got to stay *behind* your right hip. The article tells us to think of the 'reverse K' as you freeze your stance when ball is struck."

"I've heard of 'reverse C.' I've heard of 'reverse pivot.' Never heard of 'reverse K,' " I said.

"You betcha. The vertical stem of the K is the perfectly straight line of the left arm and clubshaft. The upper diagonal stem is your right arm and head. And the lower diagonal is your right leg."

"Let me try it again." I took a few swings with an imaginary ball.

"I've got to admit, it resembles the underarm toss of the skip-ping stone. That movement can feel very natural to me when I'm thinking *skipping stone,* very unnatural to me when I'm think-ing *sledgehammer.*"

I took a few more swings and grinned broadly. "Okay, I haven't fallen off the skateboard yet! "I promise to work on it. Surely we've got another candidate for Pareto here!"

We hurried off to catch up with the other pair who were waiting at the first tee.

"To find a man's true character, play golf with him."
—P.G. Wodehouse

CHAPTER 4

Disciplining the Elbows

Three days later, Harold Trittin received a call from the executive director of Laubach Literacy, an agency where trained volunteers teach illiterates to read. A special meeting of the board members was called for July 8th, the same morning of the next 'boot strap' clinic. Hal hesitated before agreeing to be there. This was a challenge to the core values and priorities he had previously defined for himself. Tugging at him was his allegiance to "pay back" to society. But equally compelling was his determination to stick to a program of skills improvement during the sunset years of his life. It didn't matter whether this was gourmet cooking, violin, surfing the Internet, whatever, but he had chosen golf. He felt uneasy suggesting a time change to me, knowing that Patti and I tutored in the central city immediately following the usual tee time. His sense of societal responsibility won out, and, with some reluctance, he gave his assurance he would be at the board meeting.

When informed of Harold's decision, I expressed admiration and moral support for making the right choice. Then I assured him I could find an unmatched partner for the competition the 8th.

As I approached the league's registration table in the clubhouse the morning of the 8th, I wondered how the pairing with an unknown partner would affect my game. Harold had been a constant source of support and encouragement. "What a true friend," I thought. "It won't be nearly as much fun with someone with whom I have little in common."

Suddenly there was a tap on my left shoulder.

"Hi! I'm told you're looking for a partner. Name's George Moore. The fellow I'm normally teamed with, Ken Hufford, is in the dental chair working on a different kind of hole-in-one."

I laughed at the witticism which immediately put me at ease. "I'm Rex. The starter told me earlier you were looking for a partner, but that you were in Division A. I'm a 'D' as in 'Duffer.' "

" 'A,' 'D.' Makes no difference to me. Who are you normally paired with?"

"Trittin ," I responded.

"Hal Trittin ? Of course! I've waved to Hal a few times, and now I recognize you as the one he's usually playing with. What a prince of a guy! When we have a few minutes, I'll tell you the impact Hal had on my life many years ago."

"I'd like to hear about it," I said. "Looks like there'll be plenty of time for that since nobody's paired with us and the party ahead is at a snail's pace."

During the first three holes of play, I found myself feeling very comfortable with this new acquaintance. George seemed to be a person who knew what he was about. It was clear he enjoyed the game and laughed off the occasional botched shot. I marveled at how he maintained his concentration. To George, each hole seemed to be a separate game, with no connection to what went on before. He was more enthusiastic about the process than the outcome. Living in the moment, he derived more enjoyment from the strategic and tactical challenge of each situation than from the achievement of a low score. No doubt this was why he carried such a low handicap, I thought.

After completing the fourth hole, the time felt right to ask about the Harold Trittin connection.

"I'll try to make a long story short," George said. "In the late '60's, I was on what you might call the fast track in a Fortune 500 company. But I was restless, impatient with the bureaucracy, and just vain enough to think I could do it on my own. With the help of a silent investor, I initiated a start-up in what seemed to be a burgeoning industry. Because things went so swimmingly for a few years, I started thinking I was infallible and began to lose sight of the fundamentals of growing a small business."

"Such as?" I inquired.

"Such as getting too heavily committed to one customer. That's where Harold Trittin entered the scene. As my banker, he was able to quickly see an ominous trend. He recognized my blindness and obstinacy in failing to act on the early warning signals. But Hal didn't give up on me. He was far more than a banker —Hal was a coach, psychologist, cheerleader and consultant. I learned more about running a business from this one man than all of the business seminars I ever attended. Then, when my major customer severed the relationship, the wheels started to fall off. Any other banker would have pulled the string at that point, but not Hal. Magnanimously, he extended our line of credit...probably taking a lot of heat from his superiors in the process. Who else would have had that kind of faith in a neophyte trying to run a fledgling business?"

"That's quite a story," I said. "Does it have a happy ending?"

George leaned on his driver and nodded in the affirmative.

"With a lot of hard work and continued support from Hal, we got the business on a strong footing. Then sold it to the same company I used to work for. It goes without saying, I'll be indebted to Hal for the rest of my life. He's one of those rare human beings who is totally and unconditionally interested in you as a person. If there's such a thing as sainthood, Harold Trittin is a first-round draft choice. More like him and our whole society would change — big time. By the way, how's Hal's golf game coming along?"

"Hal wouldn't mind my telling you it's been a struggle," I replied. "We've *both* had our struggles. But things are going a lot better since the two of us have been coaching each other on some swing techniques."

"That's great! A sort of mutual mentoring system. Maybe you wouldn't mind my making a few observations."

"Please do! I'm in the process of soaking up all the advice I can get." I said.

"Something that made a big difference in my swing was getting over the 'elbow flail.' I can't help but notice you're prone to some of that same thing. Watch how I literally 'staple' my right elbow to the rib cage throughout the downswing. With that elbow tucked in there's a sense the whole swing has a firm point of reference, an anchor. And that's just as important when chipping and putting. Only there, *both* elbows should be tucked in. Gives you a helluva feeling of control."

"That's helpful," I commented. "I'll work on that. In fact, both Hal and I will work on it."

At the next boot-strap clinic, I recounted George's description of the role Hal played in the eventual success of the start-up company.

"George Moore is not inclined to hyperbole, but he exaggerated this one," Hal demurred. "George was a super manager and the others at the bank would have squarely backed my actions. But I'm delighted you got to meet him. He's a quality guy. By the way, how's his game?"

"That's funny, he asked the same question about *your* game. He's definitely got it together. In fact, he offered some tips that were a big help to me." I described the malady of "elbow flail" and George's remedial approach to it. "He's an excellent instructor. Maybe that's why I carded my best score of the season—a barrier-shattering 98."

"Congratulations, Rex! You better have a good lesson for me today so I can catch up to you." .

"Okay, listen up!" I said. "Three things: timing, timing, and timing! Have you seen the movie, *A River Flows Through It?*"

"No, but Ethel tells me it's a must-see. Gotta get the video."

"It's great! There's lots of fly fishing in a mountain stream in Montana. When you see the video, notice how the kid brother, who's much smaller than his dad and brother, manages to cast his hook the furthest and to the exact spot he wants. So every time they fish he bags the biggest catch. It's phenomenal...more than phenomenal...it's a blend of spiritual artistry and music as the end of his line is shimmering in the sun. It gracefully dances back and forth before the final flick of his hand launches that hummer clear across the stream!"

"*That* I can visualize!" Hal said.

"This kid's strength and size has nothing to do with his effectiveness. It's strictly timing! Timing of the release of his cocked wrist in relation to the other movements. Now, I'm convinced that in my anxiety to nail that ball I'm doing two things. My arms are rushing the beginning of the downswing, and my wrists are uncocking too soon. Result: Acceleration of clubhead at impact is nowhere near what it could be with better timing. Not only that, but in my rush, the club lunges outside of the flight path. And that spells *slice* which rhymes with *vice* which means 'trouble in River City.' "

"Jump-shifting from the sublime to the grotesque, consider the fly swatter," Hal added.

"What about the fly swatter?" I asked, somewhat puzzled.

"I'm trying to prove your point about timing. When I'm doing a number on a fly, the final flick of the wrist is the key. Trying to help the speed of that fly swatter with the downward movement of the arm is a sure miss. Tightening the hands and the wrist muscles is even worse."

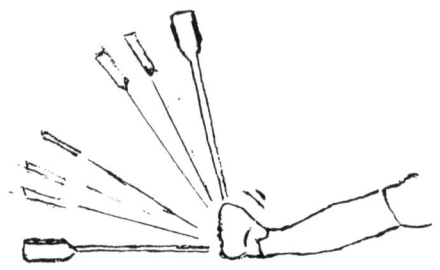

"And if a 14-inch fly swatter is quick enough to trap the fly," I added, "think about the clubhead velocity generated by the flick of the wrist holding the other end of the three-foot shaft. Surely my high school physics text had a formula for that quantum leap in velocity.

"Let's think out loud and push that one even further," I said. "All we've worked on so far suggests this kind of a model: In the swing there are two systems in play. The heavy-duty system — the feet, legs, lower body — create a targetward thrust which leverages the centrifugal effect of the smaller system. The smaller system, of course, is the 'fly swatter' — the flick of the wrists that leverages peak velocity to the clubhead. Let's think of the large system as the power generator, and the smaller system as the speed activator. And like the kid doing the fly fishing, the timing and coordination of the two systems is key to everything!"

Harold thought about this and agreed it made perfect sense.

"Yeah, in Ben Hogan's book, he talks about the different 'power gears' of hips, shoulders, arms, and finally hands, kicking in at critical intervals to build to the maximum acceleration," he said. "If one of those gears is out of sequence you've lost it. Sort of like the sequence of gears needed to rev a racing car up to maximum speed."

"Now how do you know *that*?" I chuckled. "You're going to tell me you've been-there, done-that."

"Not quite. But I *am* an authority. Saw a Tom Cruise movie with many close-ups of hands and feet as he manually shifts gears in sequence to reach top speed, then goes on to win a NASCAR race."

The synergism we were experiencing forced a spontaneous giggle. "I'm more than a little excited about our prospects for meeting our goal!" Hal exclaimed. "Hogan tells us if we focus on Pareto's 20 percent we are going to break 80! Now you've convinced us that 80 percent of the clubhead velocity is brought about by the synchronization between lower body strength and flick-of-the-fly swatter. Today's *aha* puts us on the threshold of a big-time breakthrough!"

I attempted to suppress my eagerness.

"Well, today ain't over yet," I said. "All this is a perfect lead-in to my surprise *show'n tell* for the day! Time for B.Y.O.G.— Bring Your Own Gimick. As a sort of Father's Day joke, Patti ordered this golf club velocity meter from a catalogue. This is it strapped to the end of my driver. When I fooled around with this thing, I made a remarkable discovery that confirms some of the things we're talking about!"

"Are you going to enter this as your physics project?" Hal joked.

"Guaranteed grade of A+...no, more like C+...because I can't prove the formula. But after lots of experimenting, I *can* tell you which swing dynamic gives me an 80 mile per hour reading. (Is this our day for 80's?) Now, that's within fifteen of what the pros do. Here's the skinny: What seems like a painfully slow drag at the beginning of the downswing, while my skateboard is jump-starting, in effect delays the uncocking of the wrists, i.e. flick-of-the-fly swatter, 'til my hands are below the waistline. Amazingly, this generates the highest velocity reading! It proves what we were just talking about. Flick of the wrists at the critical time in the swing is everything!"

"Fantastic!" Harold shouted.

"Of course we both know this is in conflict with how every cell in my body is genetically programmed," I said with a frown.

"Whaaat?" Hal said.

"I'm convinced every ancestor since Fred Flintstone has assumed the faster the beginning of the downswing the harder the rock is smashed. And behold! This little meter proves all those guys were wrong!"

"All you have to do is re-program the quadzillion cells of your body," mused Harold. "Sounds like the delayed gratification thing. The longer you delay the wrist snap the more gratifying the result. Your ancestors just didn't get it."

I laughed. "Is that the reason they were all lousy lovers?"

"Ahem! Well, I promise not to ask anyone. Can I tie that velocity toy on my club and give it a spin?"

"Have at it!" I said.

There were several swing attempts with the two of them huddling over the velocity meter after each. Then a short critique followed each reading. They demonstrated conclusively that in addition to critical timing, the total relaxation of muscles in the forearms, wrists, and hands translated into freer wrist-snapping and higher velocity on the meter. They also concluded that keeping the head well behind the right hip leveraged much greater acceleration.

These exercises led to an attempt to analyze the meaning of the three terms they repeatedly encountered in the instructional materials: *timing, tempo and rhythm.* Unable to agree on what the pros really meant by these terms, I decided it was only necessary to factor the idea of delayed whip of the wrists into a sharply focused image that could be easily recalled when needed. Harold, on the other hand, suggested there was something very poetic about the golf swing, and that each golfer must find his unique "iambic pentameter." This observation was not unusual in light of his fondness for literatue and the arts. The two hurried to the first tee when they heard their names called.

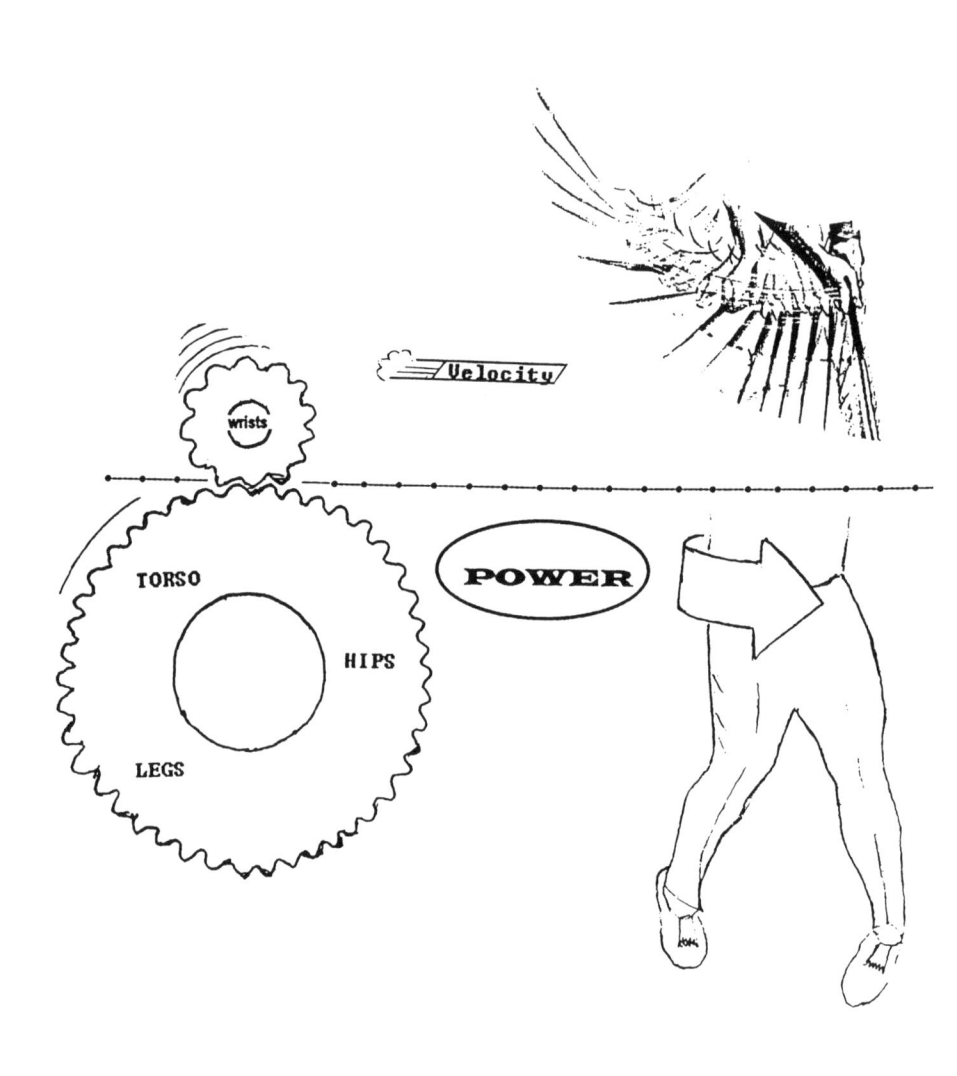

According to Ben Hogan timing of the gears is everything

"Golf acts as a corrective measure against sinful pride."
— P.G. Wodehouse

CHAPTER 5

The Perception-Reality Gap

Ninety minutes later, a break between the wrap-up at the ninth green and the tee-off for number ten permitted Hal and I to caucus without appearing anti-social to the others in the foursome.

"So how're you feeling about your progress?" Harold asked. "You seem to be in control of your drives and fairway shots. Is all the work we're doing having any impact on your game?"

"Curious you should ask," I said. "Some of the scores don't show it, but I'm feeling a lot better about things. The percentage of truly satisfying shots is much higher. My inner confidence has improved immeasurably. And yes, I attribute that directly to what we've been working on!

"For instance," I continued, "the stuff we went over at our clinic this morning is already causing a transformation of sorts. During the downswing I'm thinking 'flex' instead of 'force.' My body's flexed, my wrists are flexed. And during the first quadrant of the downswing, what used to be 'GO,' as in 'Go-for-it,' is now 'G O,' as in 'Gravity Only. That has to do with the importance of zero force on the clubhead."

"That's pretty neat, but why aren't your scores showing it?"

The Perception-Reality Gap

"Some aberrations have spiked up the scores on certain holes—wacky stuff that's beyond my control."

"For instance?" Hal pressed.

"Like the green on number three! You know, the one they built on a 35-degree hillside. This morning the surface was so crusty it resembled the penny arcade. You attempt to roll the ball into the little hole to win the ten-dollar Barney, and if you miss, your ball rolls back out of sight. I guess you weren't counting, but that was a swimming five-putt on one hole. Just a matter of unluck. I'm not going to sweat that stuff."

"That's another breakthrough, Rex, when you can shrug off five putts. It tells me you're no longer letting the negatives of the game control your attitude. Ya know, I'm reading this Tom Clancy book where Jack Ryan is having a rough time on a green like that; I call it the 'Isaac Newton Gravity Green.' Just to taunt him, his golfing partner, some admiral friend, asks him, 'You know why they named it 'golf,' don't you?' So Ryan snaps back, 'Sure I do! The S-word was already taken!'"

"Yeah," I laughed, "that's precisely the word I was trying to recall after each one of those putts!"

"Tell me, Rex, did the admirals give you a bad time on the golf courses in your earlier years?"

"Au contraire, I attribute my fast track from ensign to captain strictly to the command golf outings."

"C'mon!" Hal chided in disbelief.

"Yup, instead of reading the greens, I became very adroit at reading the body language of my bosses. Then, when the timing was just right, I would shout, 'That's a gimmie, Admiral!'"

"Too bad somebody didn't concede a couple of those suck-up gimmies to you on number three! Hey!" Hal continued, "I meant to tell you. I was at a fundraising affair at the Milwaukee Country Club Thursday night. You know how the dining room overlooks that gorgeous fairway along the Milwaukee River? Well, I was seated across from an Air Force general, and naturally the topic of golf came up. Seems he gets an occasional lesson from the club pro. He was quick to let me know that only active members could sign up with the 'master,' apparently someone with national ranking."

"Perhaps, over his career, there were too many lieutenants sucking up with 'gimmies,' " I observed, revealing my disgust.

"Yes," agreed Hal, "an ego large enough to command its own ZIP code. Said he didn't know you. Then I made the strategic mistake of telling him what you and I were up to. Unfortunately, he wasn't as charitable as your doctor friend. Scoffed at the idea that two high-handicappers could possibly elevate their games by digging it out of books and videos. But there was one redeeming thing that emerged out of that unpleasant conversation."

"I hope so," I said.

"He quoted the pro as saying it's very important for high-handicappers to be aware of the 'perception–reality' gap.

The Perception-Reality Gap

The golfer *thinks* he is performing a particular maneuver correctly when in fact he is not. Of course I didn't share this with the general, but, in my opinion, that's exactly what you and I are getting at by coming up with these exaggerated images, such as keeping the head well behind the ball on the downswing. The reality check of all this comes through loud and clear on the home video."

"Right! Let me share the perception–reality gap I suffered just last month as I was driving to Green Bay," I said. "My clear perception was that my foot was holding the accelerator to the speed limit. Later, an eighty-five dollar conversation with the state trooper put this perception in touch with reality.

"But seriously," I continued, "there's a lot to this perception-reality thing. I think of the misperceptions involved while seated in the train at the station. There's a relative movement between my train and the one on the next track. So I go into the multiple choice drill: The other train is moving forward, backward, or standing still; or my train is moving forward, backward, at rest, or none of the above. I go bananas before finally locking on to reality. So it is with the swing. The head is steady in relation to the body, but not steady in relation to the ball. Gary Player alludes to this and advises the student to consciously move the head *further* from the target during the downswing to ensure it stays to the right of the ball. He says when the head stays back where it belongs it's the fulcrum of the entire swing and leverages both power and accuracy. That makes sense when one considers the loss of counter-balance when the 16-pound head is drifting targetward, along with the lower torso, at the time of impact. At the other end of the 'seven-foot mechanical lever' is a nine-ounce clubhead traveling at 80-

plus miles per hour. That's Physics 101 that even I can understand. So I'm focusing hard on 'skull back' at ball impact. By the way, Hal, how are you doing with all this? Are you sensing any progress?"

"Definitely! Like you, there's more sweet spot connections That's my 'Nirvana.' It's a feeling of...well...sort of like a 'bliss button.' But it only comes when my mind can transcend all the mechanical components of the swing. Only then do I experience an even-flow shift of weight and perfect balance on my left foot at the conclusion of the swing. My problem, of course, is with each Nirvana, I say to myself, 'what incredible distance with so little effort! Therefore, I'll give the next swing additional gusto in order to reach Nirvana-plus-twenty.' Never works! Anyway, the confidence I'm feeling in the long game will hopefully spill over to the short game."

"I think so," I said. "If you're like me, each drive or long-iron that aborts makes me tighten-up to feeling I've got to pull off the miracle shot to make up for the yardage loss. I'm finally learning that tightening up is the worst possible thing for *any* kind of stroke — long or short. So now with fewer aborts in the long game there's much less of that. That brings up two questions: Are we going to get into the static stuff — you know, the grip, the stance, and so forth? Second, are we going to do anything at all about the short game — the kind of thing George Moore was addressing?"

"My opinion? No and yes. If the static game isn't ingrained in the DNA of the muscle memory by now, there's no hope. And yes, with the short game making up 70 percent of all strokes, we've got to put some time on it, despite the confidence spill-over from the long game. Clearly, there's a

The Perception-Reality Gap

number of differences in the short and long swings. We need a few sub-vocal sound bites to access just before each finesse shot – including putts as well."

"That raises another question," I added. "Is it time to go back over what we've done and come up with hard specifics we can work into our repertoire? I realize there's a ways to go before the whole swing is covered, but how soon can we review what we've already done, put on the Nike shoes and 'just do it'?"

"I can't disagree with that," Harold replied. "For sure we've got to focus sometime soon. But every time that thought enters my head, I get nervous about two things. First, we may not agree on the final choices. Second, in paring down to the nub of each concept, we'll probably be tossing out some marginal stuff that could be darned helpful in future exercises."

"Okay, let's wait a while longer," I said with resignation. "Let's keep plowing up the field. Eventually we'll both feel ready to make the hard selections and etch them into core."

"Thanks, Rex. Let's hope my procrastination doesn't screw up the process. Look, they're signaling us to get started."

While waiting for the others to drive the tenth, I whispered, "You'll be happy to know I already have the next candidate lined up."

"Not to be outdone, my next one is ready too!" Harold replied. "What if we were to meet a half-hour earlier next week so we can cover both of them."

"You're on! And be sure to take this velocity toy with you."

"Golf is a game of precision, not strength."
— Jack Nicklaus

CHAPTER 6

The Electrified, Petrified Left Wrist

I fairly bounded down the hillside from the parking lot, pullcart trailing carelessly behind. Hal had arrived early for our August 5th clinic. Clearly, both were excited about the prospect of exchanging new information.

"Are you ready for 'double-pick' day?" I asked.

"You bet! And it's my turn to go first!"

"Forge ahead while I get out my notepad!" I said.

"I read over and over the importance of not breaking down the left wrist at the time of ball impact. Well, my workouts tell me to extend that to about a foot *beyond* point of contact. Watch in slo-mo. The back of my left hand...perfectly square to the target...as is the face of the club. Then they both continue square to the target through and beyond where I strike the ball. When I focus on this, there's a sense of control like you wouldn't believe. Try it!" Hal insisted.

After several attempts with an 8-iron and some range balls, I said, "Sure helps. Tell me, what's the grabbing graphic here?"

"Thanks for asking. Imagine an inch-thick flat strap of steel forged to the back of your wrist when you're in the striking zone. And there's this powerful electromagnetic force —

The Electrified, Petrified Left Wrist

about 5,000 volts — tugging at that steel strap. The force is so powerful, there's no way you can hinge or even twist that wrist for the two nanoseconds the ball and clubhead are one. The vertical stem of the K — the clubshaft, back of hand, arm — are all irretrievably pulled toward the target once the ball is struck. Kinda like there's this ten-inch extension zone beyond the ball. To get my head totally into the image, I sense the 'force' when I'm first addressing the ball. I can barely break the magnetic field as I start the backswing."

The notion of an electromagnetic force consumed the depth of our imaging capacities as we hit about a dozen balls. The swings were interspersed with an exchange of observations, such as the high percentage of sweet-spot connections, an experience all of our senses detected with mystic resonance and synchronistic certainty. I broke the intensity of our drill by joking about Harold's use of the word *nanosecond*. "Until today, I was sure the only definition of nanosecond was that period of time between my clubhead locating the ball and my head looking up to ask 'wher-dit-go?'

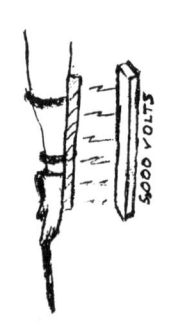

"I have to say, Hal, this one is a keeper no matter what we decide with the other finalists!"

"I'm comfortable with that," Hal said. "Now let's get on with *your* Pareto pick-of-the-day."

"Okay Hal, it's a quickie but a goodie. Twice in Penick's video they talk about taking 'dead aim' at the ball. An article

I read leads me to extend that to mean 'dead aim' at a *swath* rather than at the ball. Imagine the swath to be two inches wide and a foot long. It cuts through the grass a la Harvey's famous 'weed cutter.' Now here's the drill: The starting point of the swath varies from time to time, depending on where I want the nadir of the swing arc to be. I notice you do the same thing I do with your practice swing. You seem to align the bottom point of your swing to a broken tee or leaf. Lately, I've been repeating practice swings and adjusting my stance, or perhaps the shallowness of the swing arc, until I'm certain that swath will consistently start one inch behind the ball when I'm about to drive, right *at* the ball in the case of an iron shot. Pick your own lead distance."

I allowed a moment for that to sink in. Then I continued, "Ask me, 'Why swath, why not ball?' "

"Okay, why swath?"

"Because when the mind thinks *ball* the body's likely to slip into the *hit* mode. Remember, we're trying to convert to *throughswing* mode. Besides, the image of a swath encourages a stronger and longer follow through, and it sets the inertial guidance system for the *direction* of the downswing."

"I'll work on swath," Harold promised, "but I'm not sure it's going to command top priority."

"Fair enough," I responded. "Got time for another quickie?"

Harold glanced at his watch and signaled the go ahead.

The Electrified, Petrified Left Wrist

"This one links to something we've already been working on. Watch the s-l-o-w, l-a-n-g-u-i-d....I love that word.....movement of the first part of my downswing."

"Yeahhh!"

"Now, notice that *after* the full weight of my body is on the left foot, and *after* the swivel of the hips, I cut in the afterburner. The most aggressive part of the swing begins just one nanosecond *before* ball contact and continues into the follow-through. Result: Far more accuracy and 100 additional horsepower where it counts the most! Provided, of course, the head remains well behind the ball at impact."

I allowed another moment for focusing. "Let me elaborate on the bit about the 'afterburner.' To ensure that the centrifugal force of the clubhead is originating from my lower torso, I cross my right foot over immediately following impact. Just as though I were stepping into a put-away tennis volley, or thrusting into a full-length punching bag. Just watch. But notice also my head and shoulders don't sway toward the target the way the 'power generator' does. They stay back until *after* the ball is struck. Finally the head and shoulders are forced to move with the momentum. Until that point I'm arching my back with belt buckle thrusting toward the target in what seems like a contortionistic stance. But really, it's no different than a full-bore effort with the 'skipping-stone' delivery."

"Is this your own idea?" Harold asked.

"Nope. Culled it from the Gary Player book and the Tommy Ballard video. Also, it's the 'slingshot' part of the swing Penick talks about. The right foot crossover was made famous by Player after his back operation. Spares the tension on the spine, which is torquing like a corkscrew during follow-through. Ironically, according to Ballard, Gary's performance has improved since he got into the right-foot-crossover routine.

"According to these guys," I continued, "duffers focus too much on the downswing and flame out on the throughswing — the follow-through. This de-energizes the impact big-time. It also messes up the line of flight. The clubhead travels the arc of a circle, right? Assuming the length of your arm and clubshaft to be the radius, there's over 20 feet in the first 270-degree arc before the clubhead finally reaches the ball. Okay, that's a lot of distance for you to build up an incremental acceleration. But the climax of that force build-up should carry throughout most of the follow-through."

"Some of this sounds familiar," Harold said.

"And, oh yes!" I continued, "there's another book written by a Spencer somebody, who likens this whole concept to the launching of a rocket, if you can believe *that* one. In his vernacular, there's the ignition, booster, and sky-reach stages. Ignition activates the engine. That's the rotating crankshaft, swiveling of hips, and lateral shift of knees. Booster stage follows with the unhinging of the wrists and the lateral thrust of the extended left arm and shaft — same thing you were just describing. And, the final stage is the soaring of the clubhead as the hands reach for the sky. This guy says the vigorous action of the lower torso is in stages one and two, while the delayed aggression of the upper torso, arms and hands is in stages two and three. Now that's a lot different than my old notion of an aggressive 'slam dunk' that's all over once the ball's struck."

"Is there a resemblance here to Dr. Doolittle's 'push-me-pull-you'?" Harold asked. "Except here we have a 'pull-me-push-you.' You pull the club down with your hands and arms . Then suddenly at impact you're pushing the whole apparatus all the way up the other side —the *next* 20 feet of the arc."

"Only partially," I said. "Eliminate the word 'pull.' The first quadrant of the club's downward path should be the sensation of gravity free-fall only — not 'pull.' The second quadrant, then, consists of our 'fly swatter' — the flick of the wrists. Still no 'pull.' Thus, we've eliminated any vestige of *'slam dunk.' Slam launch,* on the other hand, is the 'push,' the all-important follow-through. I'm struck by the contrast in this approach to that of my past instructors. Their emphasis was always the mechanics of backswing and downswing. Very little on follow-through."

"Tell me more about your rocket scientist's *sky-reach*." Hal said.

"Sure. He fixes a point at the periphery and slightly above the left eyescope and concentrates totally on splitting that point with the hands. Says the trajectory of the clubshaft and flight path of ball will be just dandy if you can achieve that. Lots more control. Lots more power, too, if you laterally slide hips and legs, and shift weight completely to the left foot. And the final 'reality check' of the entire evolution is the perfect balance on the left foot at the top of the swing. Of course, I violate that part of it with my Gary Player foot cross-over."

I paused to let the image sink in. "Don't you find it interesting, that when we started out we thought this was going to be Golf Mechanics 101? Now, that's supplanted by

Rocket Science 404, with minors in Parapsychology, Kinesiology and some other far-out stuff!"

"Right on, Rex!" Hal laughed. "Just yesterday, I heard somebody describe the golf swing as a 'bundle of subtle nuances.' So much for mechanics! But somewhere underneath this whole enchilada we've still got to isolate a "bundle' of simple techniques that we can commit to muscle memory."

A sigh of resignation was emitted in unison.

"Speaking of techniques," Hal continued, "you mentioned the 'slingshot' a minute ago. That's the second time I've heard that term. Tell me what it means."

"Yeah, I was afraid you'd ask," I said. "But here's what I *think* it means. When he's in the strike zone the more advanced player injects a little more vinegar into the hit with an extra thrust or muscle spasm of his body. I choose to relate that to the buns squee...excuse me...the gunning-of-the-gluterals we talked about earlier. The metaphor with the slingshot has to do with the extra flick you give the handle of the slingshot as the ammo passes through the uprights."

"Got it. Looks like it's time to go. Say! Can I keep the velocity toy another week? It will help me prove out what we've been talking about here. Who knows, with better timing and a mental shift from slam *dunk* to slam *launch*, I'll probably exceed Mach 2 on the meter!"

"And Mach 3 if you do the slingshot," I chuckled. "Sure. Keep it as long as you like. I'll tell Ethel you want one for your birthday!"

While they strolled over to the first tee, I posed a question to Hal with some trepidation. "I don't mean to come on with a full-court press here, but would you feel comfortable coming to closure on some of these picks in the next week or two? As you know, Patti and I go to the cottage in two weeks. We'll be heavily into golf up there, so it's a chance for me to really concentrate on our final picks."

"Yeah, sure, Rex, I can't wimp out on this thing all year. We need to wrap it up. Too many word pictures and metaphors on the table."

Encouraged, I made a proposal. "How about the second clinic from now we mold metaphors into muscle memory. Ooh! Didja like the sound of that? Tell ya what. Let's take a few minutes after today's scramble to establish the ground rules. That'll save time as we individually review the candidates."

"Good idea!" Hal said. "Did you say scramble?...as in 'best ball scramble?!' I didn't realize that was scheduled for today! Do you know what this means?"

"Tell me," I said.

"You and I have a chance to star! Our golf strategy is similar. Our strengths are complementary. We energize each other. In 'best ball' we're each allowed 50 percent bum shots. All we have to do is stagger the bummers!"

"And also stagger the *winners*," I added apprehensively.

"C'mon, pal, we can do it!" Hal coaxed. "We're in for some prize money!!"

"Now you've got me pumped, partner! Let's go!"

"The first thing anybody has to do to be good at anything is to believe in himself." — Gay Brewer

CHAPTER 7

Advancement to C Division

"What a day that was!! I knew we could do it, guy!" Hal shouted, as we walked off the 18th green.

"With combined score, we're into the cash pool big-time!" I joked. "Certainly, our collective net worth jumps a buck and a half! Haven't felt this rich in a long time. Allow *me* to buy the orange juice."

In the lounge we reviewed the many H.I.T. candidates covered the previous two months. We parcelled them out according to the individual affinity felt for each. Then we agreed that the assignee would sharpen the concept into a stark and workable graphic — an image that would endure for months, perhaps years. Finally, we prioritized the picks to facilitate the final selection process.

Walking out of the clubhouse, I did an abrupt double-take on the status board posted at the door.

"Hey! The board shows we've both been elevated to C Division! Nice going partner!!" I said, gesturing for a high five.

"How about that! In my case," Hal reasoned, "it must've been that lucky 92 I tallied at the last outing. It fooled the computer into thinking I'm better than I really am."

Naw!" I countered. "I'll tell you what it is. The computer removes the worst two holes of each round, and you and I both ain't carding more than two of those ugly looking snowmen like we used to."

"Right. Well, if a snowman is an abysmal 8, then I've assembled my share of *abominable snowmen*, 9s and 10s, already this summer."

"I don't fear death, but I don't like those four-footers for par."—Chi Chi Rodriguez

"Confidence is the key to the short game."— Tony Lema

CHAPTER 8

The Short Game

"Did you work on your rocket science this week?" I joshed, as we met for our next 'bootstrap clinic.'

"Yeah, the skinny on all that was so hot I've burned it into core! Some really beneficial stuff there. But now I'm into the final phase — the short game."

"Great! Whatcha got?" I urged.

"Not very dramatic, really. Just fundamentals. But when I discipline myself to the basics the results are indeed dramatic. For starters, it's imperative that the hands are *ahead* of the ball at impact."

"Clarification," I interrupted. "Are we talking pitch, chip, putting, or what?"

"All of the above. Not only must the hands lead the ball, but the left wrist must be cast-iron-rigid for several inches beyond impact. This gets into what George Moore was telling you about, and I've been putting a lot of work into it. With the chipping and putting, the rule of both-elbows-tucked-in applies until the ball is stroked. Then your left elbow is forced to leave the ribcage as it makes a straight line toward the target. What forces this is a wrought-iron left wrist which leads the clubhead throughout the downstroke and for several inches beyond. The left elbow is then detached from the body but only *after* the ball is struck. Get the sense the elbows are guiding the stroke.

"Finally, with the chipping and pitching, make sure the lower edge of the blade squeezes...better word...*pinches* between ball and turf.

"Another drill on putting," Harold continued. "I know you've observed how many pros reverse hand position on the putter grip. I read where the main reason for this reverse grip goes like this: The conventional grip is an invitation to break the wrists just as you do with the full swing. So the unnatural feel of the reverse grip blocks out that tendency altogether. Wrists *have* to be out of play just like the pendulum swing of the croquet mallet. That's another imperative. How many imperatives can I have?"

"All you want," I said.

"Then here's a *triple* imperative! Head has got to remain still. And for me that was terribly difficult to accomplish. It only came after watching my head's shadow over and over again. Same old perception-reality thing. Thought I'd never get to reality."

"So, is that all?" I asked.

"Almost. To avoid lunging at the ball when I'm putting, I accelerate through the ball with as soft and smooth a motion as possible. For me, that not only ensures a truer putt but gives me a sense of guiding the ball during the follow-through, if there is such a thing as a follow-through in putting. Related to that, I've always prided myself in my ability to draw a straight line on a blank piece of paper."

"What's that got to do with putting?" I challenged.

"I hold my hands underneath the grip with the tips of the forefingers pressing either side of the clubshaft — the grip. I select a blade of grass 18 inches into the path for precise alignment. Then I employ the same Zen required for drawing the free-handed straight line. Voila! That's precisely the straight-line-path required to drain the ball. Furthermore, my free-hand line drawing is improved when thumb traverses the edge of the table. Likewise, the accuracy of my putt improves with my right elbow anchored to the ribcage. It's an essential guidepost, a fulcrum.

"Then, as to distance, I'm learning to *not* override the brain's intuitive judgment. We both know there's a far more sophisticated radar guidance system up there than anything the Air Force ever dreamed of. So, I carefully read the green, and with a full leap of faith, allow the brain to take over."

"Do you ever suffer the yips?" I asked.

"Sure, but Arnie Palmer has the answer to that. He suggests imagining your feet to weigh in at a ton and a half each. Miraculously, that clears the nervous system of all 'tentative-itis' and other nerve disorders. He also says the tinier the target, the more accurate and focused your brain's guidance system. Thus, after allowing for horizontal and vertical pitch and yaw of the ball's anticipated journey, select a very specific spot as the 'adjusted target.' Once selected, focus on that target only. It's too ambiguous for the unconscious level of the brain to contemplate both the hole and the adjusted target once the inputs for the latter are factored into the 'computer.' That would be an open invitation for second guessing, mental override, yips, and all those bad things.

"So, Gary Player, what do you think?"

"I think you and Arnie are right on target!" I said. "I have no quarrel with any of it. We're bound to break out of 'duffership' by concentrating on these fundamentals. Speaking for myself, there's much less mystique and witchcraft in the short game than in the swing-for-the-fences long ball. Just takes a lot of backyard practice. And, frankly, my commitment to that is stronger than ever. Let's go for it!"

"I hear you! I also hear Pareto telling us that a mere 20 percent effort involved in improving the short game will leverage 80 percent of the handicap improvement, or something to that effect."

"The golf swing is like a suitcase into which we are trying to pack one too many items."
—John Updike

CHAPTER 9

Pareto's Final Picks

Ethel Trittin's phone call to Patti led to an invitation for the four of us to get together for early dinner the following Friday at their condominium in the Cudahy Towers. "I get the idea it's very important for these guys to put their 'H.I.T.s' together...whatever that means," she laughed. "While they're conducting their seance, why don't we girls take in the movie at the Oriental." She welcomed the chance to repay an earlier dinner at our home, and particularly wanted to get together before Patti and I left for our cottage in the Upper Peninsula.

For more than an hour at the dinner table, Harold and I refrained from any mention of our research. It was as if there was a pre-planned pledge to bite our tongues in the face of this unnatural — almost painful — feeling of constraint. Unconsciously, perhaps, there was a deference to Ethel, who had obviously put an extraordinary effort into a gourmet meal of world class dimension. The elegant ambience she had orchestrated would most certainly be depreciated if the dinner conversation reverted to the topic that was consuming both of us "addicts." Though unspoken, these insightful women knew full well that at least one lobe of each of the male brains represented was saturated in golf bytes that would be downloaded with child-like eagerness as soon as the table was cleared, and spouses departed for the cinema.

The meeting was conducted with more intensity than expected. Both Harold and I were armed with the notes and scribblings accumulated over the past two months. I had prepared some sketches that captured the elements for which I was prepared. and I offered to do a finished version for our combined Pareto Picks. Furniture was moved aside to enable room for simulation of critical swing maneuvers. While there were differences in the hierarchical ranking of our picks, each of us was satisfied the techniques finally selected would meet personal needs. There was a surprising overlap in thinking processes. The models agreed upon allowed space for individual adaptations. Now it was up to each of us to focus our energies on these base points — at the driving range, in the backyard, and during odd-moment visualizations. We were confident that previous unnatural and awkward movements would ultimately meld into a natural and fluid swing. The fact that both Harold and I had already experienced a taste of this integration process was encouraging. So, too, the increased number of experienced "Nirvanas." There was a sense of hope and dedication to the intensive practice stage awaiting us that was unparalleled in our retirement experience.

However, some fundamental realities were acknowledged. For example, of the dozens of golfers who had been queried — high- and low-handicappers alike — none could concentrate on more than two things once the golf swing was initiated. Indeed, the more experienced attested to being able to discipline their minds to a state of "mental cruise control," with all thoughts neutralized. Conceding this reality, the two of us agreed that during one of two practice swings immediately preceding "live-world," a slow motion swing, ("excruciatingly slow," as Hal put it), could incorporate a penetrating review of all the *visuals* — all of the Pareto Picks. And therefore, if each visual were plumbed to its deepest recesses, then a remarkable memory residual would carry over to the entire cycle of the live swing, where a three-ounce white ball just happens to get in the way of the rehearsed swing.

Another reality: The purist would cringe at some of the exaggerated movements suggested by the visuals. He would fear the adverse effect of the "correction overkill," without appreciating the importance of narrowing the perception-reality gap suffered by most duffers.

The two of us agreed upon eight, somewhat kitschy, metaphoric labels to facilitate memory recall. Future practice swings — numbering in the thousands — would depend on this recall.

SWATH: Establishing the desired starting point and length of clubhead's "grass sweep." Opportunity to fine-tune swing arc (*V-shape* vs. the more sweeping *shallow-dish*).

SOFT FOREARMS: Complete relaxation of the wrist and hand muscles (to be maintained thoughout the backswing and down swing).

SKATEBOARD: Vigorous lateral shift of the lower torso with simultaneous SWIVEL of hips. This action kicks in the instant the shoulders have rotated a predetermined pattern (75-degree rotation minimum).

SKULL BACK: Head position remains <u>back</u> of ball until just <u>after</u> ball is struck.

STELBOW: STapling of right ELBOW to lower ribcage throughout downswing. (Ensures the inside-out swing and grooves the swing path).

SLAG: <u>SL</u>ow dr<u>AG</u> of the clubhead which ensures a delayed wrist-snap. So slow that the only downward pull on the club is <u>G</u>ravity.

SLAM-LAUNCH: The aggressive upswing portion of the follow-through. (Replaces the precarious and error-prone *slam-dunk* of the downswing).

SKY-REACH: Mental target for ultimate position of hands at the top of throughswing.

The swings of the chip shot and short pitch key on the following techniques:

STRIKE: Strike down on the ball. This calls for a swing arc approaching the shape of a V.

STELBOWS: <u>Both</u> elbows stapled to ribcage until after ball is struck.

SOLID WRIST: Left wrist (which <u>leads</u> the clubhead) freezes its position in relation to the grip as ball is struck and remains rigid for several inches after contact.

Pareto's Final Picks

And finally, the putt:

SCAN 'n TRUST: A pre <u>scan</u> of the ball path — to target and return — to initialize the brain's guidance system. <u>Trust</u> the computer" to activate the precise muscle behavior No overrides. No last-moment audibles.

SUCTION FEET: Gravity suction on feet is so forceful as to drain away all nervous system overrides (yips) that otherwise impede the brain's guidance system.

STELBOWS: <u>Both</u> elbows stapled to ribcage until ball contact.

SOLID WRIST: Sustained rigidity of frozen left wrist *following* ball contact.

Next, the two of us drew on these mental prompts, or "hooks," to choreograph the following full-cycle exercise which we facetiously labeled the "one-minute handicap reducer:"

(1) Swing club back and forth, simulating the baseball player prior to stepping up to the plate. The twofold purpose for this: To loosen up; and to observe the location of the SWATH (footprint) the clubhead is imprinting on the grass.

(2) Slow the swing down to a (painstakingly deliberate) snail's pace, which allows time to subvocalize each of the prompts in sequence: Soft Forearms — Skateboard— Stelbow—Skullback— Slag—Slam launch—Skyreach.

Consciously force the applicable body/limb components to carry out their assigned role in the prescribed sequence of swing elements.

(3) Gradually restore tempo of back and forth swings to "live world" pace, experiencing in the process a muscular coordination and body rhythm that feels as natural as possible. Step up to the ball and precisely replicate the most recent practice swing, and location of swath imprint.

Recognizing the impracticality of performing this one-minute drill prior to every long stroke on the course, we vowed to run through at least an abbreviated version once each hole, and prior to every practice shot on the driving range. Subsequently, we surprised ourselves with the short time period in which we were able to grasp a full-scale mental imaging that substituted for the physical run-through of the drill. Prior to going our separate ways Hal and I set the date of September 9th for our post-vacation critique. While apart, we individually applied the above model to countless practice swings, plus a few non-competitive golfing opportunities. We each experienced the feeling of successfully infusing into "muscle memory" our system of sequential movements that meshed into an integral golf swing — a swing so natural as to resemble a "second skin."

The meeting in September was tinged with excitement as we plunged into a detailed comparison of experiences, lessons learned, and scores achieved (a low of 85, and high of 96). Basically we both found the original slate of Pareto Picks to hold up through rigorous testing. Harold, however, discovered the SLAG prompt (slow drag of clubhead) did not adequately deal with his repeated problem of uncocking

Pareto's Final Picks

the wrists too early in the downswing. He was searching for a label that would prompt him to delay the release of the "safety" on the cocked wrists until his hands reached the plane of the right shoe. I flippantly offered *Safety Shoe* as the more appropriate descriptor, but promised to give it more thought.

Meanwhile, I discovered I no longer needed the S*oft Forearms* and S*ky-reach* prompts. The loosening-up exercise seemed to satisfy the requirement for the necessary "flex" in wrists and arms. And *Slam Launch* seemed to encompass the objective of proper club position and body balance at the conclusion of the swing.

We recorded our collective observations as to those *reinforcing aids* to the swing improvement program:

- Simulating the full swing without ever uncocking wrists enhanced the critical feel needed for the correct wrist-release sequence.

- We were each amazed at how quickly a dysfunctional swing could be self-diagnosed and self-corrected with a quick review of the Pareto prompts. Self-videotaping also helped immeasurably with this diagnosis.

- Rubber tee (purchased from any driving range) inserted into carpet sample (or large piece of cardboard) when used with the plastic ball offered a practical platform for space and time-efficient swing practice.

- Masking tape placed on the bottom of the clubhead showed streaks from the practice mat that clearly detected the errant outside-in, or inside-out, swing tendencies.

- Dabbing powder on the ball left a mark on the clubface and revealed contact position in relation to the toe or heel of the clubhead. It forced an undeniable reality as to swing accuracy.

- Backyard chipping practice with variable target distances had a remarkable influence on distance judgment.

- "Wedging" (or "pinching") the blade-edge of clubhead between the underside of ball and turf ensured a crisp connection and optimum loft of ball when chipping and pitching.

- The read of the green's undulation was greatly enhanced by imagining the tossing of a water bucket toward the pin and carefully "observing" the flow of water. Accuracy in direction was further enhanced by extending imaginary sight markers to *three*: pin, ball, and a point one foot *behind* ball. Finally, putting practice with eyes closed significantly enhanced distance judgment (the "pace" of the putt).

Pareto's Final Picks

NO!

SLAM DUNK

YES!

SLAM LAUNCH

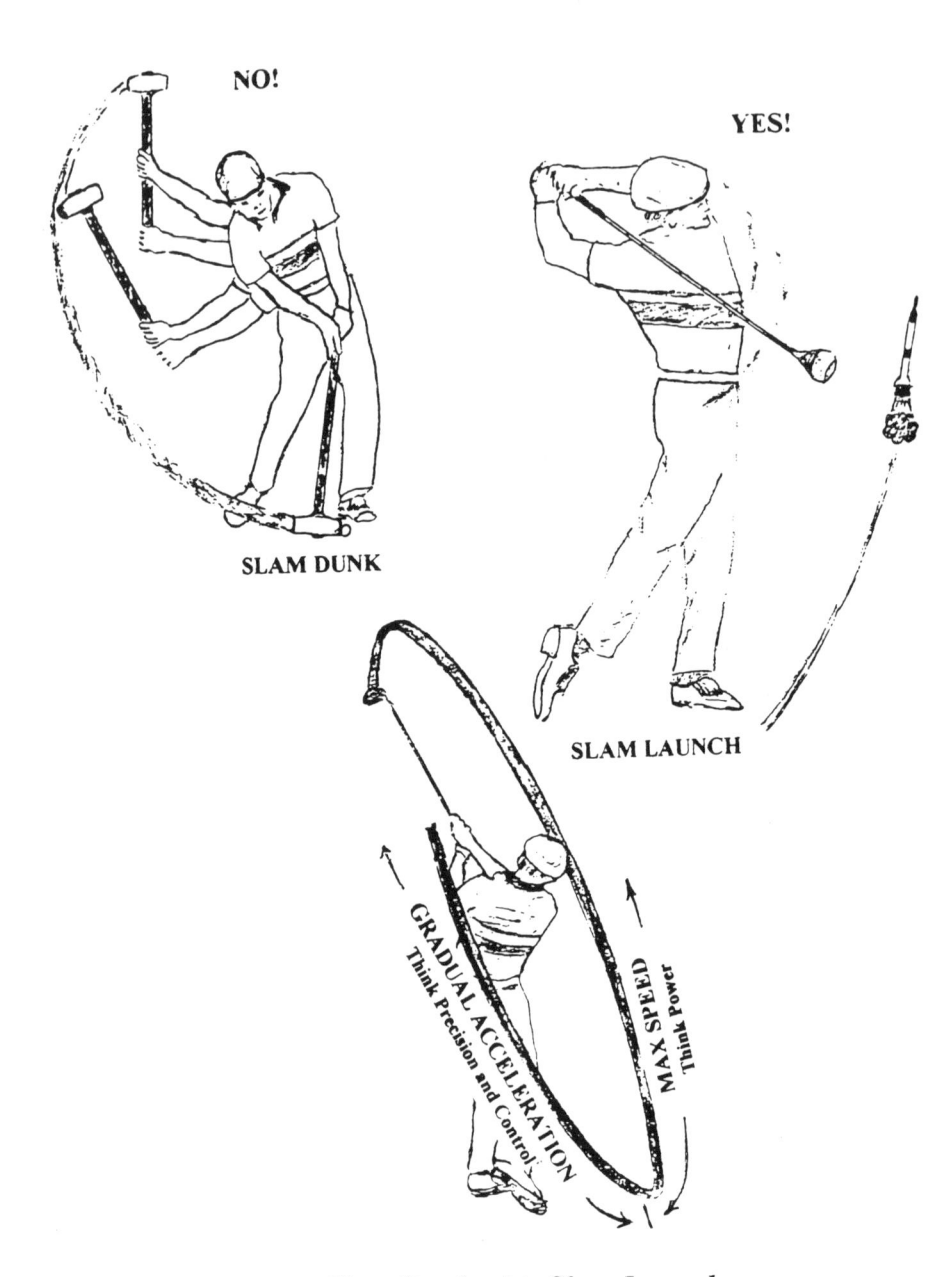

GRADUAL ACCELERATION
Think Precision and Control

MAX SPEED
Think Power

Replace *Slam Dunk* with *Slam Launch*

72

Kick-starting the skateboard triggers the downswing

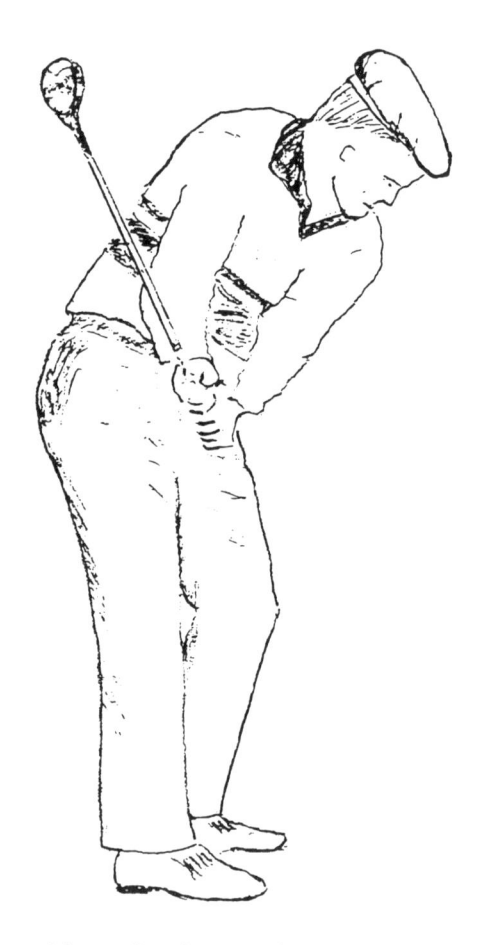

Delay uncocking of wrists until hands approach bottom of swing arc

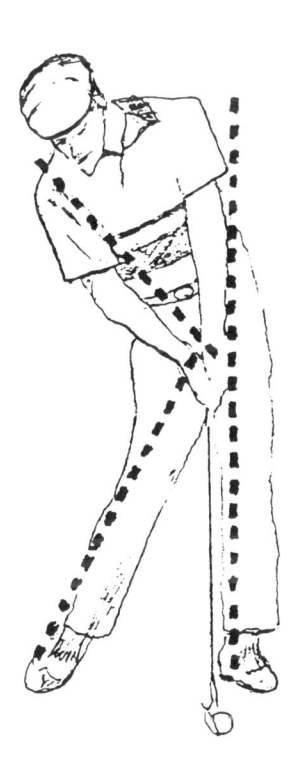

Body and club form the REVERSE K at impact

Head well behind ball until AFTER impact

Duffer's Breakthrough: To Quit or to Quest

The targetward thrust of the belt buckle resembles
the underarm toss of the skipping stone

Elbows stapled to ribcage control putts and chips

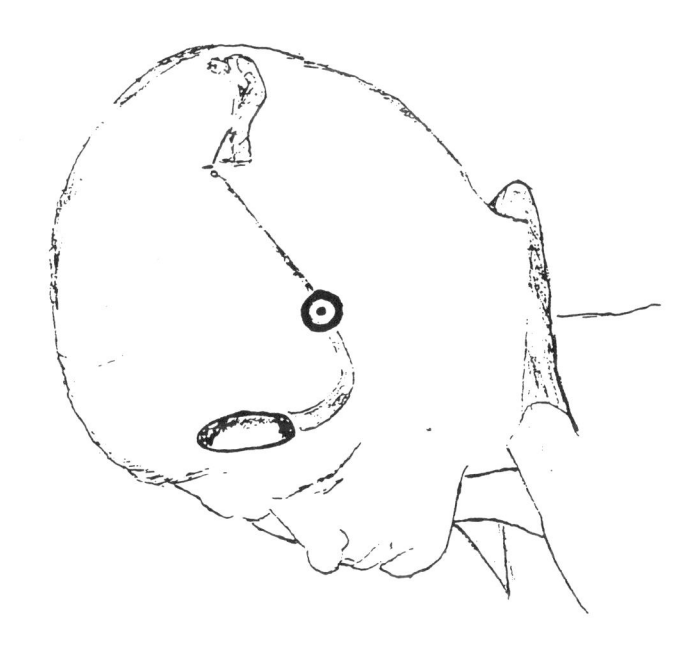

Once the adjusted target is established do not perplex the computer with additional hole-location inputs

"Golf is a spiritual game. You have to let your mind take over."— Amy Alcott

"It is not mere technical skill that makes the golfer, it is the golfing soul."— P. G. Wodehouse

CHAPTER 10

Golf and the Out-of-Body Experience

One week after our critique, Harold and I participated in the *Senior's Season Finale*. With a sunrise tee time, the first three holes proceeded extraordinarily well. There was an unconscious confluence of all the swing elements both of us had been rehearsing so zealously. Neither Hal nor I wanted to vocalize the word "zone," thinking this was a "state of sanctity" reserved for the very advanced golfer. As our foursome approached the par-five 4th, which had traditionally been My nemesis, I allowed some old negative tapes to emerge to consciousness.

"Here we are again, Hal. The fairway's so wide I can let it all hang out, right? Those trees along the right side know all about my post-traumatic-slice syndrome. One of them offered the phone number of Dr. Jack Kevorkian to help relieve my suffering."

Hal interrupted by stopping dead in his tracks and grabbing my arm. "Look at that!" he whispered in astonishment. "A doe feeding her fawns!" Each of us in the foursome froze in place and stared in awe. There was a deep sense of reverence for this poignant scene which was taking place in the middle of the fairway about 90 yards from the tee. The beauteous blend of luminous sun rays and early morning haze silhouetted the animals in a way that suggested a heavenly aura.

After a long wait and a couple of attempts to motion the doe out of the driving path, Sid Penske turned to me and said, "Okay, 'Mr. Bird,' fire away." He was obviously referring to the two successive birdies in earlier play— an unheard of accomplishment for a Division C competitor.

I turned to Hal. "You know, don't you, this represents more stress than the rookie facing the 13th at Augusta National."

"Go ahead, drive the ball," Hal urged. "You can't lose. If you revert to old form, the ball slices well clear of the dear little deers, anyway. And if you hit it solid, they'll think it's a successful satellite in orbit."

That was the boost I needed. I could not recall ever feeling more confident about my ability to execute the perfect drive in competitive play. The trepidation and second-guessing were unexplainably absent. After a rehearsal swing, complete with repertoire of visuals, I was able to put my mind in neutral. No secondary thoughts about mechanical dos and don'ts. Only a sense of fluid motion. It was as if a higher self outside the body had taken over the responsibility of integrating and blending all the positive ingredients of the seamless golf swing.

The deer were not disturbed by the flight path of the ball, which was on a prolonged trajectory as if guided by invisible streamers until it finally came to free fall just short of the creek. This was a hazard usually negotiated in the second fairway shot with B and C Division competitors. Prompted by the drive's extraordinary distance, the shouts and cheers from the others, including the foursome behind us, who by now had noticed the deer, were enough to prompt the deer "threesome" to the edge of the fairway.

As soon as Harold had a chance to catch me alone, he probed, "Now don't give me the 'aw shucks' routine. What *really* happened back there?"

"It's hard to explain, Hal. Something to do with the out-of-body experiences in that book, *Golf in the Kingdom*. We've talked about Murphy's book before and wondered if anything that mystical-magical could really happen. Suddenly it seems more plausible."

"Can you be more specific?" Hal asked.

"Only to say there was a quiet exaltation that seemed to overtake me. Do you recall the part where Shivas Irons describes the 'feeling force' that embraces the inner body, the club, the ball, the intended flight path, and even the universe? I experienced something like that. It was as if my deeper mind was outside my body imaging the ball's trajectory and making it all happen."

While waiting for the next foursome to clear the green at the par-three 5th, Sid Penske strolled over to me and slapped my shoulder. I couldn't help but wince under the sting of the slap, and wondered what underlying emotion might have induced such a blow over what I assumed to be a friendly gesture of congratulations.

"That drive back there... huge!" exclaimed Sid. "Say! What's with you two, anyway? Ned and I were paired with you guys a couple of times last year when you both were performing like real hackers. Suddenly you've got it together! What gives? Tell us your secret!"

Hal and I caught one another's eye. Then Hal deciphered my grin to read, "You go first. I can't handle it just now."

"You're right, Sid," Hal began. "There *is* a secret. And we're glad to share it since you asked. You've heard of Pareto and the 80-20 rule?"

"Prato. Yeah! Wasn't he the Japanese fellow who shot an 80 in last year's U.S. Open but finished the tournament 20 strokes under par?"

"Different guy. This Pareto was Italian and did his thing circa the 1925 Open. Let me try again. A while back, Rex and I decided we were going to master the mechanics of the golf swing — either figure it out or quit the game altogether. We soon discovered that to make the swing a predictable exercise we had to formulate some visualizations in our head to discipline the routine. Now, Rex here discovers there's another element to the game involving some out-of-body experiences. So when you..."

"C'mon you guys, get real!" Ned Ghormley sharply interrupted Hal. "Visualizations? Out-of-body experiences? Golf can't be that complicated. People who try to make it a head game probably need a head adjustment themselves! Go ahead and drive, Sid. Let's finish the round."

Nearly out of earshot, we could hear Ned mumbling to Sid about the stupidity of equating golf to "psychological folderol."

Hal turned to me and said, "When am I going to learn to read the questioner before answering the question? Shucks, I didn't even get to tell Sid and Ned about the nuances of the swing, Nirvana of the sweet spot, and a bunch of other 'folderol.' Sorry, partner, if I embarrassed you back there."

"The click of the solid shot soaring far down the fairway is well worth all the hours of practice." —Jimmy Demaret

CHAPTER 11

Nirvana and Goals Reviewed

Leaving the 18th green, we were ebullient as we eagerly located our favorite table in the clubhouse lounge where we could savor the highlights of the past four hours. Tink! The encounter of two fresh orange juice glasses was meant to prompt a toast. But I interrupted Harold's celebrative gesture by an impulsive outburst, "Ah, sweet Nirvana! That's the same 'tink' my titanium driver makes when the sweet spot kisses the ball!"

"Patti's right," Hal said, shaking his head. "You've definitely become a golf-a-holic when the clash of juice glasses reminds you of your driver. Tell me, does this addiction replace the other addiction you told me about three months ago?"

"You're referring to my uncontrollable urge to crush the ball?" I experienced a fleeting moment of nostalgia that was laced with both sweet and sour. The negative feelings of revisiting that devastating affliction were offset by the profound sense of relief in knowing the crush-the-ball demon had, itself, finally been crushed. The foe was vanquished. "Naw, no more addictions in my life! Not even golf."

"Whatever you say, pal. I'll be your reality check on that one from time to time. So where are we? No more duffership? Goals achieved? Or, are we still a work-in-progress?"

"All of the above," I replied. "I'll never again answer to 'hacker.' But the work-in-progress continues— as a fun sort of thing— without the humiliation and the exasperation. I'm just beginning to see why people stick to this crazy game."

"Really?" Hal said.

"Yeah. There's more than the sound of 'tink' out there. There's an unexplainable sound of music. Every so often at the symphony a score will seize me at both the emotional and spiritual levels and lift me up. And so it is on the fairways when the trees, turf, ball, and self all come together as one entity. Exhilarating! Is that too mystical? Too much 'folderol?'"

"Yeah, but I'm identifying with it. *All* of it!"

They both paused to savor the significance of this revelation.

"And what's your take on all this, Hal?"

"Hard work, but lots of laughs. Frustrations fraught with angst— soon overcome by a series of mini-victories and a satisfying sense of achievement."

"Hmm, that's the stuff that sparks personal growth," I said. "I suspect I've been a beneficiary of some of that growth these past few months."

"In what way?" Harold asked.

"Oh, I suppose I'm a person with more self-confidence. Easier to laugh at myself. Less hard on myself. Now I know I can master any skill within reason. Didn't used to believe that—not really. Who knows, if I can gear the golf swing into cruise control, maybe I can get into the same flow at the piano. You know, the same kind of uplifting music I hear at the symphony."

"Aha! Piano lessons replaces golf?" Hal chided.

"Nope. I'm enjoying this game too much now. I like the instant feedback with each stroke. The chance to correct—hopefully to improve. The challenge that a microscopic correction in the swing can make a sea-change in the sustained flight of the ball. The constant hope and anticipation of the perfect shot."

There was a lengthy pause during which each of us, now the closest of friends, were in mental rewind to the early weeks of the season when we confessed feelings of near hopelessness over our inability to improve.

I continued, "You once mentioned the fellowship. I've thought about that. Seems that in the tumble and humble of the game, you get to know the totality of the human beings you're playing with. After the first few holes they strip themselves of the usual roles and masks they're wearing. Someone once said, 'Real fellowship only takes place where there's total honesty—openness to the point of vulnerability.' Golf somehow nurtures all that. A person's reaction to someone else's small victories, and the golfer's reaction to his own setbacks reveals a ton about what's underneath.

"I've also thought about Shivas Iron's observation about golf serving as an 'x-ray to the soul.' It brings out so many sides of a person's psyche—almost a journey to enlightenment."

Nirvana and Goals Reviewed

Harold had to take a minute to take that all in. "Heady stuff, that."

After a few moments, I said, "You're the goals guy, Hal. What lofty aspirations are you harboring for the next chapter in your golfing life?"

"Right. Well, the choice is clear. Either it's goal-setting and *wear out,* or forget the goals and *rust out.* I never thought I'd break one hundred. Now we're both in the mid to low-90s. Can't speak for you, but I'm already lusting for the 80s. How's that for a lofty aspiration?"

"Go for it, Hal! Let's make a prophecy right now: By this time next year we're both in Division A. Not only that, but Ethel and Patti have both gotten into this seductive game and are showing signs of enjoying it! Now you can't get any loftier than that with a sand wedge."

Harold Trittin gazed out the window while contemplating that thought, as well as his own vision for consistently shooting in the 80s. He was struck by the beauty of the 18th green. The color richness was accentuated by the white, pure-quartz sand of the bunkers surrounding the green. It resembled an emerald mounted in a diamond setting. In the background, the lush fairway meandered down the hillside through the gauntlet of mature hardwood trees along the rocky creek. The sight was so intoxicating he barely took notice of the excitement over a 42-foot putt tenaciously in pursuit of the hole. The ball was following a tortuous path on the sloping green. Finally, the satisfying sound of "ker-plunk" trumpeted a birdie 4 on Brown Deer's second most difficult hole. The celebrating foursome was just finishing their round, and ...yes!...the player with the hot putter was George Moore.

Hal shifted his gaze directly on me. "It's strictly up to us, pal, whether these fantasies translate to sweet Nirvana, or merely another batch of Ned's 'folderol.' "

"Golf is a game of integrity."— Raymond Floyd

EPILOGUE

Though the league play had officially ended, Hal and I continued to get together weekly until the end of an unseasonably mild November. Most of the public access courses throughout Milwaukee's northern suburbs were explored for their unique challenge and for the splendor of autumn colors. We continued charting our scores, net of charitable mulligans, and surprised ourselves by the number of mid- to high-80 scores we were achieving. Had these been tracked on the league computer the numbers would most certainly have merited a Division B standing. As "former duffers" we eagerly anticipated our probable progress throughout the following summer. Sustained scores in the low- to mid-80's no longer seemed out of reach.

Unfortunately, our golf round of November 23rd would be Harold Trittin's last. Fifteen weeks later he underwent open-heart surgery. His liver had been weakened by hepatitis years earlier which contributed to his inability to survive this invasive surgery.

Losing an occasional friend or relative was not unusual in this stage of my life. But the usual feelings of grieving and questioning, bordering on self-pity, were somehow different with the loss of Harold Trittin. There was an unexplainable sense of peace. A sense that things were okay. I didn't try to analyze the reason for this, but I had an opportunity to describe this feeling of serenity and assurance at a chance meeting with George Moore while browsing the book stacks at the North Shore Library. George's genuine interest in my response to Hal's death inspired me to be perfectly open about these feelings.

"And what exactly do you think Hal would have you do about the successes you experienced together?" George inquired.

"I frequently sense Hal's presence — especially when I walk by his memorial marker in the birch grove next to the North Shore Church. But I've got to tell you, George, we haven't reached the medium communication stage just yet. No seances that I'm aware of."

George pressed again. "Okay, what do you *think* Hal would have you do?"

"Knowing how goals-oriented he was, I think Hal would urge me to do two things. He would have me document the steps we went through so others could share in the same quick access to the improved golf swing. And, for sure, he would urge me to compete in next year's league so as to prove that what we worked on together was more than a passing drill."

"Well, I don't know whether this reinforces Hal's wishes, but it's interesting that I was about to call you to ask if you were available to be my partner this summer. Seems Ken Peters, my partner the past two years, is moving to Arizona. He and his wife are convinced the links get more sunshine out there."

"Sure, George, I'd like that very much! I'm sure Hal is okay with that. But I'll check with him at our next seance."

While I was quite sure my game would resume at about the performance level of the previous fall, I was surprised to see my handicap continue to drop at a deliberate pace. And late in the season's competition I was astonished to see my name on the Status Board under Division A. It was clear to me that the ongoing encouragement and mentoring of George Moore was a significant factor in this accomplishment.

The same day the new division assignments were published, I managed to birdie the par-three 5th. After applauding this feat, George shouted excitedly, "You realize, don't you, this is hallowed turf! Same hole that Tiger Woods 'aced' the first day he turned pro!"

"Yeah, I'm aware of that," I said, as I mimicked Chi Chi Rodriguez with my putter and "scabbard." "But here's the thing: At our first successful seance with Hal, he's going to confess to the big screw-up. It was ordained that Rex Coryell nail the hole-in-one, and that Tiger settle for the bird!"

Fully aware of what the Division A assignment meant to me, and what it surely would have meant to Harold Trittin were he alive to participate in the fun, George hosted a small and informal lunch at the Town Club for the foursome that played together through most of the season.

This time I chose not to interrupt the toast when I heard -the celebrative "tink" of glasses.

George announced, "To Rex, the newest member of Division A. Duffer no more!"

I attempted to conceal a sudden rush which momentarily seized my entire psyche. "Thanks George." I paused to regain my composure. "And here's one to the 'Gipper!' In a very real sense, Hal was a Division 'A'er all his life. Now in that Greater Reality, he's shooting with the masters."

Acknowledgment

The idea for the book was inspired by Harold Trittin (now deceased), golfing partner, dear friend, and former officer of Associated Banc-Corp. But bringing the project to fruition would not have been possible without the inspiration, encouragement, and advice of a cadre of coaches and cheerleaders: Benefactors of "no-excuse" golf clubs—the CEOs of TEC Group 17; friendly naggers Ken Huff, Armour Swanson, and Harry Dennis; literary advisors Gary D'Amato, Cynthia Dennis, Richard Pauls, Jeff Coryell, and Bob Kuhns; golfing advisors Rudy Duran and Eric Coryell; strategist Steve Quale; and loving counselor Patti Coryell. I am profoundly grateful to each!   R.C.

About the Author

Rex Coryell held 12 diverse assignments in the U.S. Navy, including commanding officer of a supply center, prior to his retirement in 1971 with the rank of captain. He subsequently served as assistant headmaster of an independent school, assistant to the business school dean of an urban university, and senior associate of an international organization that conducts executive education and personal counseling for CEOs. He is a graduate of Annapolis and the Harvard Business School, where he co-authored two case studies dealing with the tapping of human potential. Currently, his energies are devoted to church activities, central city initiatives, and reading. Another activity called *golf* threatened to become a *bane* and a *blight*, but recently blossomed as a *bliss*. Rex and his wife, Patti, live in Milwaukee, Wisconsin. They have five sons and five grandchildren.

Notes

Notes

Notes

Notes

endorsements continued from back cover

"A superbly written and well illustrated primer for both golfers and golfer wannabes." — **Tom and Dorothy Taylor**, Marquette Golf and Country Club

"*Duffer's Breakthrough: To Quit or to Quest* is truly a win-win book. First, it's a great way to enhance a duffer's game using well-tested techniques. Second, it adds value to the lives of disadvantaged children through the Golf Foundation of Wisconsin / First Tee. Rex's approach to the book and its proceeds reflects his Christian character and very generous heart."—**Tim Hoeksema,** CEO, Midwest Express Airlines

"I was enthralled by the way the two pals in Coryell's story arrive at 'Quest' over 'Quit.' Those of us that have spent a lifetime pursuing golf's *holy grail* can easily identify with their efforts. If you love the game and have ever experienced the thrill of hitting that rare perfect shot, this book will hit one for you. My partner and I— both mid-handicappers aspiring for better—are absorbing the contents and will take it from here!" —**Byron Higgins**, Lincoln Hills Golf Club

"Past attempts at golf have led me to the conclusion a decent and consistent swing is unattainable. Now that I'm pretending to be in semi-retirement, I'm giving the game one more try. My first scan of *Duffer's Breakthrough* leads me to conclude there is hope — even for this duffer. Some very clear tools are there to groove me into positive mind-sets and constructive habits."
—**Frank Shrontz**, Chairman Emeritus, The Boeing Company